# Playback

# PRAISE FOR *PLAYBACK*

"*Playback* is a breezy, informative history of the continuing dalliance between music and machines."
—*New York Times*

"Comprehensive, well-researched and thoroughly engaging . . . *Playback* traces the development of musical technology from wax cylinders to iPods and revealingly illustrates how, with each new innovation, reactionary forces in the business panicked, cried wolf and tried to shut it all down."
—*Chicago Sun-Times*

"Dissecting 126 years of recorded music through the prism of technology is no easy task, but Coleman manages it admirably . . . *Playback* is full of fascinating riffs on sound machines, from Edison's phonograph to Apple's iPod."
—*Rolling Stone*

"A sharp, static-free overview of the evolution of audio technology."
—*Boston Herald*

"Short and sweet . . . consistently excellent and authoritative."
—*Publishers Wee*

"[Coleman's] expertise in the area of popular music s' through . . . may well be indispensable."
—*Library*

M A R K

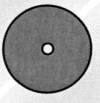

# Playback

*From the Victrola to MP3,*
*100 Years of Music,*
*Machines, and Money*

C O L E M A N

**DA CAPO PRESS**
A Member of the Perseus Books Group

3/11/08
Lan
$15.95

The Library of Congress has cataloged the hardcover edition as follows:

Coleman, Mark, 1957-
    Playback : from the Victrola to MP3, 100 years of music, machines, and money / Mark Coleman.
      p. cm.
Includes bibliographical references (p.  ) and index.
    ISBN 0-306-80984-2 (hardcover : alk. paper)
    1. Sound recording industry—History.   2. Music and technology.   I. Title.
ML3790.C65 2004
621.389'3'09—dc22

                          2003024998

First Da Capo Press edition 2003
First Da Capo Press paperback edition 2005

ISBN-10 0-306-81390-4 (pbk.)
ISBN-13 978-0-306-81390-0 (pbk.)

Published by Da Capo Press
A Member of the Perseus Books Group
www.dacapopress.com

Da Capo Press books are available at special discounts for bulk purchases in the U.S. by corporations, institutions, and other organizations. For more information, please contact the Special Markets Department at the Perseus Books Group, 11 Cambridge Center, Cambridge, MA 02142, or call (800) 255-1514 or (617) 252-5298, or e-mail special.markets@perseusbooks.com.

*Text design by Jeff Williams*
Set in 10.5-point Sabon MT by the Perseus Books Group

*For Susan and Miles*

# CONTENTS

# ACKNOWLEDGMENTS

MY DEBT TO THE WRITERS, editors, engineers, producers, scientists, and academics credited in the bibliography is gigantic. Their visionary body of work forms the core of *Playback*.

Tribute must be paid to the tireless staff of the the New York Public Library of the Performing Arts at Lincoln Center. At the library's temporary home on West Forty-third Street, I was afforded space to plug in my laptop day after day with no questions asked, and every one of my arcane and convoluted queries was answered. The story of popular culture in America resides in this amazing collection.

Exhibiting the patience of a saint, Leonard de Graf at the Edison National Historic Site let me examine rare documents and unearthed precisely the vintage photographs I needed.

My debt to my editor, Ben Schafer, is incalculable. Without his questions and guidance, musical sense, and literary sensitivity, *Playback* would be tangled up in my head somewhere. Thanks for all your hard work.

Thanks to Andrea Schulz for taking that first leap of faith, and to Jane Snyder for reading my first draft.

## Acknowledgments

Counting accomplished writers among your friends certainly doesn't hurt when you're writing a book. Still, nothing could have prepared me for the generous response of my colleagues and confidants. David Fricke provided a staggering flow of source material, finding crucial texts for several chapters. And special thanks to Susan Klimley for steering me to Ray Kurzweil's "Life Cycle of a Technology." Chapter 8 wouldn't exist without David Browne. David donated voluminous notes and files on the subject: a treasure chest of facts, anecdotes, leads, tip-offs, and juicy tidbits. Betsy Israel graciously came to my aid with a model for my bibliography. Thanks for the photo tips, too.

I wouldn't be able to write a word without the support and guidance of my family. Larry and Lee Ramer, my second parents, offered tons of emotional support along with a clean, well-lit space to work. Your generosity truly knows no bounds. The interest and encouragement of the rest of my immediate family kept me going for four long years. Thank you to John, Nancy and Gary, Stephanie, Doug and Michelle for never tiring of asking the question, How's the book going?

Simply put, *Playback* would not exist without Susan Ramer. As my literary agent, Susan has every quality a writer needs: tact, insight, integrity, and determination. She fought for this project every step of the way, offering solid editorial and commercial advice and maintaining enthusiasm when the going got tough. And as my wife, Susan was obliged to live and breathe *my* book even when she wasn't at the office. Throughout this incredible balancing act, she never faltered. Susan helped me formulate my book while keeping the focus on our family life. I couldn't ask for more loving inspiration.

## Acknowledgments

Sadly, my most loyal and least critical readers won't get to see this book. My parents, James and Mary Louise Coleman, left me a great legacy: a love of literature, boundless intellectual curiosity, the courage to question conventional wisdom. And my uncle, Thomas Coleman, paved the way by being the first writer in our family. My only regret is that you all didn't live to read this acknowledgment.

# INTRODUCTION

SUDDENLY, POPULAR MUSIC RESEMBLES an alien landscape. The great common ground of the last fifty years or so now looks strange and forbidding, perhaps even treacherous. Of course, the *music* constantly changes. Take the most obvious example: To ears raised on rock—that is, attuned to melody and alert to message—the rhythm-defined sound and defiant stance of current hip-hop registers as a grim and impenetrable throb. This is part of a time-honored tradition; parents aren't expected to understand their children's enthusiasms. But the current crisis isn't about evolving musical tastes, abrupt stylistic shifts, or even the long-delayed graying of the Pepsi Generation. Rather, today's generations divide over *how* they listen to music, not what kind of music they enjoy. In the twenty-first century, radical advances in music technology threaten to overshadow the music itself.

The changes have been rapid and unsettling, pervasive and somewhat perverse. Prerecorded music no longer arrives enclosed (or embalmed) in a prepaid plastic disc. The iconic album format is obsolescent, if not already obsolete. Compact discs, the solid gold standard of music delivery, suddenly seem clunky and redundant (not to mention obscenely overpriced). That sacred shrine, the stereo system, has been dismantled if not defiled, its function consumed by the all-conquering home computer. For a new generation of listeners, pop songs represent yet another choice on a limitless entertainment menu: more eye-reddening text aglow on the monitor screen.

Controlled by conglomerates and corrupted by payola, radio stations stifle consumption of the very commodity they once stimulated: new music. The Top 40, never exactly a democratic model, is now a crushing totalitarian state run by the self-fulfilling prophecies of focus-group surveys. Meanwhile, the once-mighty music business suffers through a painful, involuntary, and prolonged makeover. Now weird scenes occur inside the record company diamond mine, and the light at the tunnel's end is distant and growing dimmer by the minute.

What happened, exactly?

By summer 2002, the music business was in turmoil. A dip in CD sales set off tremors of dread about the future. *USA Today* delivered the initial shock wave on June 5. "For the first time in Sound Scan's 10 years of tabulating album sales, 2001 represents a year-to-year decline." Three months later, the *Wall Street Journal* echoed the full resonance of the downturn. "World-wide music sales totaled $39.8 billion in 1996, but were down to $33.6 billion last year [2001]." The same *Journal* report, on September 6, cited another ominous statistic. "For the first time since 1966, no album sold 5 million copies in the U.S. last year." Perhaps the record moguls' worst fear really was coming to pass. Their young customers were losing interest in prerecorded pop music. And they were growing more bored, restless, and distracted by the minute.

Toward the back of the chorus, the *New York Times* reported that sales of blank CDs outnumbered recorded CDs during 2001. That statistic is telling. Don't forget that until 1998 or so, blank CDs were a useless commodity to music consumers. Even the most high-end CD players lacked a record button. For the first time ever, consumers now take the lead in deploying new entertainment technology. They're circumventing corporations and redefining copyright law in one huge digital group grope known as *file sharing*.

## CD Equals Compact Disc, Controlled Delivery, Certain Death

Prerecorded CDs have been compromised, devalued. Album sales sag because the album format is exhausted. People are tired of the package. The commercial appeal of packaged music itself is in question. Home computers have liberated recorded music from the record. No longer dependent on a single enforced software format, consumers are free to choose.

With crystal-clear 20/20 hindsight, we can see that the end result of the CD boom was an inevitable bust. The abrupt transition from vinyl LPs to compact discs stimulated the music business like nothing before or since. After 1991, vinyl virtually disappeared. So consumers bought lots of replacement CDs for their old LPs and cassettes, along with the latest releases. The compact discs did sound better, or different; they cost a few dollars more, too. In the end it was self-defeating. This forced upgrade demeaned the intrinsic value of recorded music while increasing its sticker price. Short-term profits preceded long-term losses.

Notice how the digital music technology isn't driven by some elusive notion of better sound. The quest for sonic perfection—high fidelity—is a definite nonstarter in the Internet age. The very term *hi-fi* survives only as nostalgic kitsch, a dated remnant from the era when cars sported aerodynamic tail fins. Perhaps the search for the Holy Grail of high fidelity ended with the CD. One truism of digital music already seems obvious, that people will settle for *decent* sound—something less than state of the art—as long as the price is right and musical selections are vast and unfettered. Freedom of choice is the engine powering the Internet music revolution.

Music downloading thrives on the Internet, and not only because it's free. (File sharing also requires vast reserves of patience, perseverance, and a high-speed connection.) The main attraction is unlimited scope, endless selection—a musical buffet for growing appetites. The diverse, far-flung, and data-saturated nature of the Internet stokes this feeding frenzy. If CD equals controlled delivery, then sheer amplitude defines Net music. Eclectic tastes are stimulated by an endlessly shifting menu, and vice versa. The tight, narrow-cast focus of traditional music marketers and the so-called broadcasting industry increasingly misses the point. Napster and other file-sharing schemes aren't just about stealing music; file sharing encourages listeners to pursue hunches, check out tips, indulge whims, and develop new enthusiasms.

In the digital age, no single style or "sound" can dominate and define pop music as it once did. Indeed, the logical conclusion of this digital adage troubles most middle-aged rockers. While perhaps hard to accept, pop music is no longer the cultural focus of adolescence and young adulthood, an emerging person's picture window on the world. It's simply one choice among many. Popular music—rock included—is in the process of conceding its primacy.

Threatening as it appears, however, this turn-of-the-century digital coup represents a necessary shake-up of the music business. What looks to be the end of something is rather a new beginning. Yet none of this happened overnight. The downloading boom, the Napster debacle, the CD sales crash, and the authoritarian monotony of radio are fully anticipated by events in the not-so-distant past.

Meet Public Enemy Number One: James Caesar Petrillo, head of the musicians' union, the American Federation of Musicians (AFM), during the 1930s and 1940s. During the birth of radio in the late twenties, Petrillo emerged in Chicago as the working musicians' advocate. From the start, he loudly labored as the sworn opponent of records—*canned music* was his pejorative tag. Playing records on radio put live musicians out of work, end of story. James Caesar earned his middle name. Petrillo battled for retribution: he demanded high royalty rates and threatened strikes, and finally pulled off a big one in the mid forties. It was self-defeating in the end. Petrillo's crusade yielded short-term gains, at least in the hectic postwar period; but the wave of technological innovations such as stereo, tape recording, and LPs washed his power base aside. James Petrillo died in 1984. It's a pity he didn't live to hear the record industry unload on Napster and file sharing in much the same way he denounced canned music. The echoes are pitch-perfect.

## The Big Playback

Initially, the whole idea behind recorded sound was to *imitate* live music, to reproduce "natural sound." Beginning with Thomas

Edison, however, the act of recording profoundly affected the resulting sound of music. Those "natural sounds" were gradually transformed, absorbed, or abandoned. Today the distinction is meaningless. Recorded sound is utilized in concert halls and theaters; even orchestras and opera singers indulge in electronic amplification. More important, recordings are assembled, or mixed, from other recordings. Pop music is continually feasting on itself.

From the very beginning, the power of certain voices was actually enhanced by the peculiarities and distortions of the recording process. The great tenor Enrico Caruso offers the most spectacular example. At the turn of the twentieth century, Caruso sold millions of records around the world. "I Pagliacci Vestila Giubba (On With the Play)" from 1907 is a leading candidate for the elusive title of the first million-selling disc. While the figure may never be verified, it seems accurate: the Caruso phenomenon also sold lots of record players. According to the historians Oliver Read and Walter Welch, "he was the best salesman [the Victor Co.] ever had."

Bass and soprano voices, though, were too much for the early recording process: the highs were too high, the lows too low. Tenors fared better; the full shape of their voices could fit into the narrow range of the horn. And Caruso's supple tenor came roaring back out. He communicated absolute mastery and telegraphed overwhelming emotions. His sonic impact was such that he stood six feet from the horn when recording. He belted, but *sensitively*. Caruso also projected the seductive power of charisma—his voice radiates warmth in tones that are personal, intimate. His popular four-minute arias established the prowess of grand, slightly melodramatic singing on record.

## Introduction

Technology has always shaped popular music. Physically shaped, that is—duration of recording is a defining factor. The design or format is dictated by technology, yet the format can also dictate musical form in a thousand subtle ways. Popular music today might be liberated from the strictures of one physical format, but it remains shackled by listeners' similarly shaped expectations. The three- or four-minute pop song isn't going anywhere (and the big bands are coming back).

For the music industry and customers alike, the central issue today is playback. Music machines that don't record are playback-only, from the classic phonograph to your quickly aging CD player. Music machines that can record or copy sound as well as play it back—tape decks, home computers, various digital players—have always been perceived as a financial threat by the recording industry. This is not an ungrounded fear.

The back and forth over playback-only is a traditional, time-honored feud that goes back further than one might think. Conventional wisdom decrees that Thomas Edison invented the phonograph in 1877. In fact, Edison's pioneering sound-reproduction machine didn't spin a turntable, as there was no disc. Instead, Edison's phonograph played a can-sized object called a *cylinder*, laterally turning it like a rotisserie, pulling a needle through tinfoil grooves. More important, Edison designed his phonograph to make recordings as well as play them back. It was primarily intended to be an office dictation machine, not a music player.

The modern disc-spinning turntable can be traced to Emil Berliner, who patented his first playback-only gramophone in 1887. After a decade of trial-and-error competition with Edison and others, Berliner's failing business was absorbed by the Victor Company. By 1906, his gramophone morphed into the Victrola, the first successful mass-market record player. Though Berliner never saw much money for his effort, in many ways he bested Edison in terms of future influence and impact. Edison didn't quit the music business until 1929, and by then he was a beaten man in many respects. Edison no doubt was the superior inventor, but he lacked the marketing skills then required to make it in the shark-infested waters of the record business.

In the nineteenth century, recording technology struggled with format (discs versus cylinders) and function (music versus dictation). Now people demand music discs that will *take* dictation. In the twenty-first century, music businessmen have ceded control of the forward technological rush and relinquished it to their (former) customers. After 100 years or so, a century-plus of runaway profits, the big playback is played out.

## The Rise of the Nonmusician: Dick Clark Is the Father of Puff Daddy

During the early 1940s, American phonograph record plants actually shut down for a couple of years. One problem, along with the AFM strike, was a wartime shortage of shellac, the basic material in 78 rpm records. Derived from secretions of tree insects, shellac had to be imported from India. World War II thus got in the way of record production.

Once the war ended, it was a different story. Wartime research in surveillance and communications yielded groundbreaking peacetime applications in recording and radio. The age of high fidelity began with a visionary Hungarian-born scientist toiling away in the CBS electronics laboratory. Not only did Dr. Peter

Goldmark find a synthetic replacement for shellac (he employed synthetic vinylite, or vinyl, to make lighter, better-sounding records), but he also invented the 33⅓ rpm long-playing album, known as the LP. A classical music buff, Goldmark always claimed his driving inspiration was the desire to hear major works without interruption. (Similarly, compact discs were designed to run seventy-five minutes because a Japanese engineer loved Beethoven's Ninth Symphony.)

In today's light, Goldmark might be best described as an engineer rather than inventor—or maybe inventor-for-hire; at any rate, he was a corporate employee. Goldmark worked for CBS for thirty-six years, much of that spent running the lab. And as a corporate inventor, he naturally had to satisfy a mercurial boss, in this case, the legendary William Paley. So Goldmark wasn't required to be a self-starting entrepreneur in the sense of multi-taskers such as Edison or Alexander Graham Bell. He didn't need to seek funding for his ventures, though he did have to shepherd his projects through the corridors of company power. Perhaps he didn't have to sweat the bottom line quite as much. He could afford to see himself as a purist, a man of science above the commercial fray.

With the massive CBS support system behind him, Goldmark applied a laserlike focus to his work. Inevitably, corporate priorities collided with scientific vision. Goldmark developed competitive technology for color TV and videotape early in the game (or so he claimed), only to be squelched by CBS. Yet there's no doubt that Paley marshaled the full weight of the company behind the LP. There was no other choice.

The LP also inspired a competing format. RCA, headed by Paley's rival, David Sarnoff, responded with 7-inch 45 rpm records. By the early 1950s, the fight was on. The ensuing tug-of-war rocked the music business. Think VHS versus Betamax, with a different outcome. After several years of combative ads and confused consumers, the infamous Battle of the Speeds resulted in a truce: the peaceful coexistence of both vinyl formats set the stage for the coming rock 'n' roll explosion.

At the same time that technology shaped music, it spawned the music business. A so-called major label had to manufacture and distribute records as well as produce music on them. During the rock 'n' roll era, businessmen started to influence music as much as did musicians and machines. The music business had always furthered the ambitions of nonmusicians. By the fifties, they were asserting—or assuming—a creative role. Take Dick Clark, the ageless TV presence who built a financial empire behind the long-gone *American Bandstand* dance show. Before the payola scandal, the young Clark owned stakes in everything from music publishing and production to record manufacturing. He had it all covered. And of course, Dick Clark began as disc jockey.

Here was the job where businessman and technician merged with artist: a little entrepreneur, a little engineer, a lot of entertainer. Actual musical knowledge or ability was a plus, but not usually necessary. Disc jockeys (or DJs) are the key players in our story, as they are the instigators. DJs were the first nonmusicians empowered to make music, thanks to the miracle of recorded sound and the mendacity of the music business. The influence of the DJs can be charted in three successive waves.

The *commercial innovators* ruled between 1948 and 1965; they were radio DJs who wielded the seductive clout of the Top 40. They influenced (and exploited) musical tastes while encouraging sustained consumption of records and record players. The *musi-*

*cal innovators* labored from 1965 to 1979 or so; the original disco DJs mastered the art of selection—that is, anticipating and stimulating the club crowd's tastes. Eventually, they created a mass audience. Disco DJs changed how records were played and how they were made. The *technological innovators* emerged in 1973 and persevere today: With two or more turntables, they treat recorded music as raw material and redefine the notion of a record player. Hip-hop DJs employ the turntable itself as musical instrument.

The tide turned in 1979. Disco sounded the death knell of the record business, not the music business (not yet, anyway). The earth trembled when Donna Summer released "Love to Love You Baby" in 1975. The extended 12-inch single of this sexy chant echoed the rhythmic repetitions of a club DJ. Disco tested the limits of acceptable sexual content and the recording format itself. Incredibly, the disco craze ultimately backfired on once-cunning record company moguls. Their business was never the same again. Compact discs offered only brief respite from the technological upheaval. The early 1980s battle over home cassette taping neatly portends the file-sharing revolution some twenty years later. What goes around comes around.

WHY WRITE A BOOK about music and technology? Because I took tech for granted; I didn't think twice about it. Then the Internet phenomenon caught me, a music maven, completely unawares. Look away and eventually, inevitably, the next generation—of both people and machines—leaves you in the dust.

Oddly enough, I was part of the machine, a cog in the pop culture trash compactor. Covering pop music as a journalist, I reviewed hundreds of albums and wrote about hundreds more in various formats. For fifteen years I processed—listened to—thousands of LPs and CDs. Yet for all that time and study, all the divining of musical influences and invention of journalistic angles, the impact of technology barely registered. I assumed it was dull. It turns out I was wrong.

Music technology asks us to take it for granted. The intoxicating magic of sound reproduction springs from the transparency of the mechanical process. Means of delivery fades as the music plays. It's so sleek and efficient that you don't notice the technical marvel on display, by design.

This book was born as a biography of the turntable, an attempt to identify the phonograph as the driving engine behind a century of popular music. The more I delved, the more the history of a single machine became the story of machine-made music and those who made it possible, from the Victrola to the Internet.

For more than a century, beginning with Edison's 1877 demonstration to the editors of *Scientific American*, trade publications and specialty journals such as *Billboard* and *High Fidelity* have documented events and innovations typically glazed over by general-interest magazines. Read past the scandal mongering and legal theorizing in the business section of the newspaper and you'll find some devastating accounts of the decision making that shapes technological formats. Study it long enough and the systematic marketing of recorded music—what Joni Mitchell branded "the star-making machinery behind the popular song"—looks like a triumphant human extension of technology.

Consider the following divination published by the late Lillian Roxon in 1968. An Australian journalist based in New York, Roxon combined the sensibility of a gushing teenage fan with the instincts of a seasoned tabloid reporter. This eerie reverie comes from her book, *Rock Encyclopedia*.

Some people believe that by 2001 rock will be entirely machine-made. Machines will be programmed so that combinations of different sounds will be left to chance. At-home listeners will have controls that will make it possible for them to "produce" a record—speed it up, slow it down, make it louder and softer, and separate the tracks, adding, subtracting, overdubbing—to create their own version of a hit. There will be no live performances, no stages. Music will be heard with a small circle of friends, not a group of strangers.

Understandably, technological change is often viewed as a threat; but that perception can change, too. Technology is only intimidating until you learn how to use it. In the end, I believe that technology *enhances* music. It begins with a human touch and ends with the human ear. Machines don't make music unassisted. Somebody—a person—still must program, produce, perform, and play the stuff. We haven't written ourselves out of the equation yet—and we still hold the ultimate power over recorded music in our own hands. We can always turn it off.

## chapter 1

# MAGIC IN A TIN CAN

BEFORE THE TWENTIETH CENTURY, listening to music was a temporal, fleeting experience—and a rare treat. In America, most often it was heard in church and perhaps at home, if someone had talent, not to mention a piano. Marching bands would strut down Main Street on national holidays; enjoyment was a civic duty. Symphony and opera concerts were the preserve of urban highbrows. Burlesque and wildly popular, the comic songs in vaudeville and minstrel shows thrilled the nineteenth century's popular culture—the lowest common denominator. The invention of recording, the phonograph, brought them home.

Sound reproduction didn't instantly change the nature of music, but the invention of the phonograph and the introduction of phonograph records gradually transformed our basic relationship to music. Technology to a large extent determines what we hear and how we hear it. The compact (three or four minutes) duration of the popular song is the enduring result of technology devised by Thomas Edison and others. Since playback is brief, popular songs must be instantly recognizable. Then as now, faced with the novelty of new technology, listeners crave the comforts of familiar music.

The phonograph domesticated the public spectacle of amusement in the early 1900s. From the beginning, technology turned popular culture into a moneymaking proposition. Penny arcades, or amusement halls, were the first place most people attended the miracle of sound reproduction, via coin-operated machines that presaged the jukebox. By the early twentieth century, the home phonograph was being marketed as an affordable miracle, a poor man's luxury. The existence of leisure time itself was a novelty at this point, a by-product of the Industrial Revolution. The subsequent rise of tech-generated entertainment marks the beginning of the Information Revolution.

Music machines have always led the charge in information technology. For all its technical beauty and smarts, the phonograph conveys something deeper, a magical power; music cuts to the emotions, communicating on a profound human level. Still, a little perspective is in order regarding music and machines. However miraculous it seems, the act of making music is but one application of technology. It's easy to be myopic about this; just as there's more to life than music, there's also more to technology than music. Especially today, in what seems like the too much information age, it's easy to get swept away by hype. Take the computer. With its vast capacity and lightning-quick speed, it's capable of a great deal more than reproducing sound or providing a communication network. In the twenty-first century, music isn't driving technology, it's domesticating innovation, just as it did with another wondrous contrivance, the phonograph, 100 years earlier.

Technology evolves. It regenerates and improves, much as we do. Modern-day inventor Ray Kurzweil builds machines that bridge the gap between technology and music. Kurzweil sets flexible criteria for measuring this progress. His "Life Cycle of a Technology" lists seven stages. *Precursor* is the pie-in-the-sky phase of daydreams and plans. *Invention* means the moment of creation—actual birth. *Development* marks growth and refinement, including some additional creation. *Maturity* is when a technology appears dominant—and indomitable. *Pretenders* signal the emergence of a rebel technology, a challenge that is ultimately repressed. *Obsolescence* is when the successful coup takes place, toppling a sleeping giant. *Antiquity* is the end of utility—when technology enters retirement.

Technology and music too have merged in Kurzweil's life history, to great effect. As a high school student, he appeared as a contestant on the TV quiz show *I've Got a Secret*; he played a piece of piano music that was actually composed by computer—one that the young man had built and programmed. In the 1970s, Kurzweil invented a reading device for the blind, print-to-speech via computer. Stevie Wonder bought one of the first Kurzweil Reading Machines, and he consulted with the inventor when Kurzweil turned to making synthesizers in the 1980s. Kurzweil claims his synthesizers emulate the complex sound response of the grand piano: a resonant acoustic sound, not the tinny processed sound of an electronic organ. When it comes to music, technology also presents limitations—or at least they sound like limitations to older ears.

The life cycle of the phonograph closely follows Kurzweil's criteria, with a few novel twists. Record players reached maturity during the hi-fi fifties and stereo sixties. Tape players and prerecorded tapes—remember 8 tracks?—represented the pretenders challenge during the seventies. Obsolescence took hold in the eighties. The popularity of cassettes—prerecorded and blank, for portable players and home taping—consistently chipped away at the dominion of the disc. The compact disc coup caught us by surprise in the early nineties, nearly overnight, or so it seemed.

Most important, the turntable found a new purpose in its twilight years. Antiquity has been postponed: the good old phonograph did not go quietly. Turntables are now widely recognized as a musical instrument, the driving force behind dance music and hip-hop.

This refurbished position stands in stark contrast to the rusty status of the typewriter, for instance. A rough contemporary of the phonograph, the typewriter emerged in the late nineteenth century. Replaced by computerized word processing in the mid 1980s, typewriting became an early casualty of the digital era. The mechanical rain of clanking keys is long gone, replaced by a steady, subliminal *tap tap tap*. The concept of a keyboard survives, however. Unsurprisingly, it began on the piano.

The invention of the player piano, or pianola—an automated instrument—runs roughly parallel to the phonograph. The player piano essentially played itself. It was powered by suction, pumped by foot pedals, programmed by tiny perforations on interchangeable rolls of paper, and played by felt-tipped wooden fingers pressing the keys. The pianola was patented by Edwin Votey of Detroit in 1902. Votey's first model stood in front of a standard piano; later versions (and competing designs) enclosed the playing mechanism within the piano. The Wurlitzer Company of Cincinnati introduced a coin-operated "nickel-in-the-slot" player piano in 1898, capitalizing on the phenomenon of public amusement. Player pianos remained popular until 1930 or so—right around the time that radio threatened to eclipse phonograph records. Yet the phonograph survived, while the player piano didn't. Why? Singing to the accompaniment of a player piano couldn't compete with listening to sophisticated sound recordings. Still, player pianos filled a niche. According to the historian Russell Sanjek, "eventually 75,000 player pianos and a million music rolls were sold." And the player piano crudely prefigures the sampling keyboards of the 1980s. Feed 'em the right program and a recognizable sequence of sounds will emerge. Thanks to technology, you don't need to be a musician to play a musical instrument.

## Patent Wars

> The history of technology is full of instances of similar inventions being made simultaneously by two or more different groups.
>
> —Bob Johnstone, *We Were Burning*

Inventors rely on patents. Granted by the U.S. government, patents insure ownership and right to profit from an invention. The United States Patent and Trademark Office (USPTO) grants patents for protection of inventions; a patent for an invention is a grant of property rights to inventor. Today, a patent holds for twenty years from date of application. According to the USPTO, a patent guarantees "the right to exclude others from making, using, offering for sale, selling the invention or importing the invention into United States." Patents thus do not protect the right to make, use, sell, or import an invention. Patents extend the right to *exclude others* from doing so. This distinction is crucial, as is the following caveat. Patents are granted for a demonstrably working machine or process—you can't patent an idea or suggestion, a design or outline.

Patents began in England under the reign of the Tudors. Queen Elizabeth I (1561–1590) awarded monopoly status to key traders and manufacturers, a corrupt system that was scrapped and revamped during the next century. Starting in 1718, "specification," or proof, was required of patented inventions. Watt's 1796 patent for steam engines set an important precedent: patents would be granted for improvements on an already-existing invention. As the Industrial Revolution spread from Europe to America, the competition for patents went through the roof. Anybody, it seemed, could aspire to be an inventor.

The competition in information technology was especially fierce, even at the very beginning, when patents provided potent legal ammunition for battling pesky competitors. The telegraph battle matched American and British scientists. A U.S. patent was granted to Samuel F. B. Morse in 1840. Britain declared the patent invalid, instead recognizing the electric telegraph of locals William Fothergill Cooke and Charles Wheatstone. The telephone, of course, is synonymous with Alexander Graham Bell. He was granted a patent for it in 1876. Bell, however, and competitor Elisha Gray filed on the same day—February 14. Bell got the nod and walked home with (possibly) the most lucrative patent of all time.

Without question, Guglielmo Marconi is considered the father of radio. In 1897, he was granted U.S. patent number 586,193. But he continually faced stiff competition from Edwin Armstrong and

Lee De Forest; in the years to come, Marconi's U.S. rivals both won key patents.

Philo T. Farnsworth, though, *ought* to be known as the father of television. He was granted a patent way back in 1930. Thanks to an industry boycott of Farnsworth's technology, enforced by RCA's David Sarnoff, that early television patent expired in 1947. The ascendance of commercial TV networks quickly followed. Patents still provide legal ammunition in the technology struggles of the twenty-first century. Jeffrey Bezos, CEO of online retailer Amazon.com, was recently granted patent 6,029,141 (along with three other people) for single-click Internet shopping.

When young Thomas Edison applied for his early patents in the 1860s he relied on the services of a patent lawyer. Negotiating the bureaucracy has always been arcane, demanding labor. Obtaining a patent was expensive in those halcyon days: total fees exceeded $35, and you had to submit a working model and detailed blueprint of your brainstorm. Any dispute with another inventor or "infringer" incurred additional fees. Decades later, Edison threatened to work around the whole process by holding his own "trade secrets." By 1888, he could get away with it.

The age of invention and inventors properly begins in nineteenth-century Europe. Michael Faraday and Bernard Ohm laid the groundwork for electricity; Henrich Helmholtz and Jules Antoine Lissajous pioneered the science of acoustics. There were others. Many of these visionaries constructed their inventions as theoretical abstractions—"pure" scientific research. Yes, some of them were wealthy amateurs, glorified dilettantes. Characteristically, American inventors pursued a more pragmatic path. They were interested in applications—business applications. Their inventions tended to *work*.

Inventors were the technology entrepreneurs of the late 1800s; successfully promoting your invention required equal parts engineering skills, business acumen, and all-American showmanship. The go-go years, those heady days of runaway innovation and warring inventors, roughly extend from 1880 to 1910. The phonograph epitomizes this era, the age of invention. Competition was key. Edison reached his sonic breakthrough by expanding on the experiments of his peers and predecessors. In the wake of Edison's first patent, the phonograph was further refined and improved on by competing inventors.

Unlike many European geniuses, Thomas Edison understood that marketing and manufacturing skills were central to the public success of his products. And he backed up his boastful predictions and publicity with solid workmanship. According to Oliver Read and Walter Welch, the phonograph was a simpler, more efficient invention than the telephone. "From the start, [the phonograph] worked much better." The phonograph merged cutting-edge technology with mass-market salesmanship, paving the way for twentieth-century pop culture.

Just as several inventors (or businessmen) can lay claim to a single invention, more than one *format* can serve the same technological purpose. Size, form, and shape—the overall style or presentation—determine the format. The dimensions of a book jacket, the length of a television program, the arrangement of data on a computer disc are all defined by format. Within a developing technology, when one format challenges another for dominance, it's a fight to the finish. Heated competition arises, human passions ignite, and commercial pressure fans the flames. Invariably, the fire sets off a format war.

## Magic in a Can

> There are, of course, many people who will buy a distorted, ill-recorded and scratchy record if the singer has a great reputation, but there are infinitely more who will buy for the beauty of the recording with fine voices, well-instrumented with no scratch.
>
> —Thomas Edison, 1915

It wasn't always there. The multimedia monolith we call the entertainment industry began as a simple machine: the phonograph, or record player or turntable. Originally, the phonograph was a crude device with a profound purpose: a rudimentary mechanical rendering of a sophisticated idea. That crackpot dream—reproducing the human voice—inspired too the invention of the telephone and telegraph; but the phonograph quickly became more than a means of communication.

Music made the phonograph a revolutionary medium, the spinning machine that drove pop culture to its current position of dominance. And American popular music, the sonic outpouring of immigrants, vulgar and vernacular, provided the phonograph power to change the world.

The success and evolution of the phonograph wasn't the result of one man's singular genius or vision. And it was hardly a group effort. The phonograph was the product of intense competition between many individuals: inventors and investors, fakes and flukes, hucksters, hopefuls and hacks, scientists and artists and businessmen. Even the wizard himself, Thomas Edison, didn't anticipate or appreciate the full impact and influence of his invention. When the phonograph failed as a stenographer's tool, Edison turned to music reproduction with mixed results. According to his biographer, Paul Israel, Edison consistently valued technical advances over artistic quality. He concentrated his business on phonograph manufacture rather than record production. "But as the novelty of hearing recorded music wore off and customers began to pay more attention to the artists and their music," writes Israel, "Edison began to face considerable competition because he failed to recognize that music recordings involved art as well as technology."

Edison underestimated or misread the phonograph's potential, though he pursued the business well into the 1920s. By that time, the phonograph was no longer his "baby," if it ever had been. A master inventor and a genius self-promoter, Edison managed to permanently attach his name to a machine he didn't create single-handedly.

Edison publicly demonstrated his first working phonograph in 1877. Adeptly courting the media, Edison unveiled his machine at the New York offices of *Scientific American* magazine. One year later, with patent in hand, he incorporated the Edison Speaking Phonograph Company. Note the whole name. When he started selling his phonographs in 1877, Edison viewed them as dictation devices for the business market, a quick and efficient means of transcribing correspondence.

Edison wasn't the first inventor with that notion, either. Edouard Leon Scott de Martinville, proud Frenchman and amateur scientist, invented the phonoautograph in 1857. It was a recording device based on the flexibility of the diaphragm, though it didn't reproduce sound. The phonoautograph used a stylus to trace sound vibrations—on paper. Also in France, the poet Charles Cros proposed a protophonograph of sorts: his invention could record and reproduce sound on disc. Cros presented a paper to the Paris Academie de Sciences in 1877—the same year of Edison's miracle invention. Since Cros didn't construct a model, we'll never know if his dream machine worked.

## The Bell Connection

The vibrating action of the diaphragm is central; Edison first conceived the idea of sound reproduction while playing a Jew's harp. Around the same time that Edison unveiled his first phonograph, Alexander Graham Bell developed the telephone. Where Edison worked on a machine that would transcribe sound waves onto a pliable surface and then reproduce them, Bell devised a means of transmitting sound waves across wires. Friendly competitors they weren't, though their efforts were complimentary. After Edison patented his first phonograph in 1877, Bell and his associates sought to improve on it.

Teaming with his cousin, Chichester Bell, and the engineer Charles Sumner Tainter, Alexander Graham Bell wanted to develop a user-friendly—and commercially viable—version of the early record player. Flipping the word *phonograph*, they came up with *graphophone*. It was patented in 1886. They felt it offered consumers an easier-to-handle machine. Edison, who'd busied himself inventing the electric light for several years, returned to the fray around the same time. Bell and company tried to recruit him into their camp around 1887 and were rebuffed. They were willing to share their technical improvements, their financing, and patents—in exchange for a piece of the profits. But this early media conglomerate was a nonstarter. Unlike the computer mogul Bill Gates 100 years later, Edison was not interested in absorbing his competitors; he wanted to erase them. Edison declined any and all offers to merge or join forces with other inventors. "Let the best one win" was his unwavering philosophy. Accusations and patent-infringement suits flew back and forth like crossfire. Bell's financial backers went on to establish the Columbia Phonograph Company in 1888. Actually, neither device—the Edison phonograph or the Bell graphophone—caught on with consumers in exactly the manner intended. As dictation devices in the workplace they were disasters, clumsy and impractical.

## Penny Arcades and Playback

Like many pioneers, Edison and Bell were blind to the full significance of their discovery. Perhaps their considerable attentions were divided; multitasking can't be easy when you're busy inventing the future. Astonishingly, Edison defined the vanguard in a dozen varied fields, from electricity to cement manufacture.

But Edison was also partially deaf, figuratively and in fact; he consistently underplayed and misread the musical potential of the phonograph. He strove mightily to improve his "favorite invention," but much to his chagrin, others would perfect and profit from the phonograph.

One reason lies in the recording format: the software, in modern parlance. Until the 1920s, Edison staked his reputation on the cylinder phonograph. A German-American engineer named Emil Berliner invented the disc phonograph, later called the *gramophone*. Berliner is the true father of the turntable, what we recognize as a record player. Born in 1851, Emil came to Washington,

D.C., from Hanover, Germany, at age nineteen. He studied physics at the Cooper Institute (now Cooper Union) college in New York City. During a subsequent period of employment in fledgling Bell Labs, at one point Berliner saved Alexander Graham's bacon. The up-and-comer invented a telephone microphone, putting Bell ahead of his arch rival, Western Union. (The telegraph company was considering entry into the phone market, with Thomas Edison supplying the tech.) Berliner applied for a patent for his laterally recorded disc gramophone in 1887, a full decade after Edison's phonograph had appeared. The basic patent for the gramophone (no. 564,586) was issued to Berliner in 1896. The turntable was born.

The Edison phonographs utilized cardboard cylinders wrapped in tinfoil and turned on a hand crank; the stylus etched vertical grooves into the foil. The graphophones used vertically etched wax cylinders instead of tinfoil, which made for better fidelity. Eventually, Edison switched to wax cylinders. More important, both the Edison phonographs and Bell graphophones could record *and* play back cylinders; how could they take dictation otherwise? Berliner's system, however, couldn't take dictation. The gramophone was a playback-only machine—and that made a big difference.

Another crucial distinction between cylinder and disc rests in the recording process. Berliner's process allowed for the creation of a master recording. Eventually, this practice led to the mass production of records: an unlimited number of gramophone discs could be stamped from a single master recording. Manufacturing an equal number of Edison cylinders required a bank of recorders and many repeated takes in the studio. It soon became apparent that musicians and consumers clearly preferred discs.

What finally captured the public's attention were phonograph demonstrations at carnivals, in amusement halls, and penny arcades. If not for its novelty appeal, its entertainment value, this celebrated scientific advance would have disappeared from public view before the turn of the century. In 1889, a San Franciscan named Leon Glass invented an attachment that allowed the phonograph to be coin-operated. Around the same time, Glass obtained display space in the Palais Royal Saloon; he set up a coin-operated phonograph with prerecorded cylinders. Music supplied the main draw.

People lined up by coin-operated record players, donned a pair of stethoscopelike earphones and *listened*. These primitive jukeboxes carried a menu of sheer entertainment: popular songs and opera arias, comic routines and dramatic recitations, marching band music and sentimental ballads. Suddenly, a legitimate demand for phonographs—and prerecorded cylinders—materialized. By 1891, one thousand of these nickel-in-the-slot machines were emptying America's pockets. After the Chicago Exposition (World's Fair) in 1893, coin-operated phonographs exploded into a full-on fad.

Before that, the phonograph field was stagnant. Early in the decade, Edison assumed control of the North American Phonograph Company. But this venture with investor Jesse Lippincott quickly went south in the souring economy. His New Jersey plant—Edison Phonograph Works, if you please—was soon reduced to making voltage meters and voting machines. By 1894, North American Phonograph slid into bankruptcy. Edison took a powder, and his patents. Two years later, he wheeled out the new and improved National Phonograph Company.

At the same time, Berliner worked to improve his gramophone. At first, the flat metal discs were coated with rubber. Improving durability and sound, Berliner switched to a shiny mix of shellac and limestone. Finally, he settled on a hard plastic called Duranite. A spring motor powered the gramophone, as in a sewing machine. Edison's early machines used a crank. The gramophone discs measured 7 inches wide, played on one side, and ran two minutes in duration. The sound quality, according to contemporary popular opinion, was inconsistent at best: discs ran a distant second to cylinders. Truthfully, neither format caught on as a consumer item.

The 1890s posed a challenge. Edison delivered on his "trade secrets" threat, selectively applying for patents and keeping everything he could under wraps. Infringement suits were hurled in every direction throughout the fledgling industry. Berliner got caught up in a patent fight with American Graphophone, charging that its so-called vitaphone was a blatant gramophone knockoff.

During this troubled infancy, an eccentric figure named Gianni Bettini emerged on the phonograph scene. He contributed something more than comic relief, however. Born in Novara, Italy, in 1860, Bettini wound up marrying a wealthy American socialite named Daisy Abbott. Subsequently, the couple made a splash on the New York City social circuit. A former cavalry officer in the Italian Army, "The Lieutenant" was a sharp-dressed man who sported his old uniform on special occasions. He also indulged an unlikely scientific streak: Bettini bought an Edison phonograph in 1888 and set about "improving" its sound quality. As an inventor, he's strictly the Don Quixote of the phonograph. He developed and marketed the *micro-phonograph*, a stylus attachment for the cylinder machine. Alleged to improve sound quality, his supercharged needle enhancement never amounted to much, commercially or technically. Rather, Gianni Bettini's fame (or notoriety) stems from his boundless enthusiasm for music—and his relentless pursuit of recording. He literally recorded anyone passing through the family who seemed "interesting." At a Bettini bash, apparently, every other guest was an opera singer. He amassed a magnificent catalogue this way, including soprano Nellie Melba and other great names of the day. From all reports the sound quality was inconsistent. (Very few of the Bettini cylinders survived World War I.) By selling his cylinders of famous opera singers, Bettini forged the three-pronged connection between creativity, technology, and commerce. He was the first music mogul.

## Format War One: Cylinder Versus Disc

America's urban population was growing, and it represented the ideal audience for this music machine. The U.S. population almost doubled between 1880 and 1910: immigration and urbanization thus combined to create a vast and varied market for recorded music.

Of course, there were plenty of diversions to fill this void; the advertising industry grew right alongside the phonograph business. A later version of the disc-spinning gramophone, the Victrola, became the popular industry standard because it was more aggressively marketed than the Edison phonograph. That classic illustration of a terrier listening to a phonograph horn—"His Master's Voice"—became one of the first unforgettable ad hooks.

Ironically, the dog logo began life back in 1894 as a painting of Nipper and an Edison cylinder phonograph! Five years later, faced with a new patron and a new recording format, artist Francis Barraud brushed in a disc-spinning gramophone next to the hound.

The Victor Talking Machine Company was formed in 1901, uniting Emil Berliner with the engineers Eldridge Johnson and F. W. Gaisberg. Johnson was a New Jersey machinist who had been supplying the clockwork motors for Berliner's gramophones. Wisely, Johnson sat out the patent wars. He snapped up the trademark for "His Master's Voice" in 1899, and then bided his time until the Victor deal. "One of the very early types of talking machines was brought to the shop for alterations," he recalled years later. "It sounded like a partially educated parrot with a sore throat and a cold in the head, but the little wheezy instrument caught my attention and held it fast and hard."

Though the sound quality of its Victrola was arguably inferior to the Edison cylinder phonograph, the disc player had some distinct advantages: it was self-contained and easier to operate. The speaker horn was totally enclosed within the cabinet. Handily, the Victrola also featured internal storage space for discs. Now the phonograph would be designed, decorated, and marketed as if it were a piece of furniture. Compared to the can-shaped cylinders, the flat discs were easier to store, package, and handle. From this point forward, the phonograph settled down in the living rooms and parlors of America. At $200, in 1906, it was a serious investment, though not out of reach for many. The Victrola played at a slightly louder volume than the cylinder machines, and its discs were easier to store. At first, all discs were 7 inches wide and ran for two minutes. After 1903, Victor began releasing selections on multiple formats: 8, 10, and 12 inches. Playing speed—rpm, or revolutions per minute—was adjustable, varying according to recording speed. Larger discs meant longer duration and better durability. In time, more discs were available. In the marketplace, the sheer quantity of discs trumped the superior sound quality of cylinders.

The most prominent champion of the disc format was the opera tenor, Enrico Caruso. In 1902, he declared that he would record only on discs, and subsequently became the first superstar of recorded music—the original platinum artist. Caruso was also the first musician to pull in a royalty for each record sold. At the beginning of the twentieth century, the popularity of Caruso and other opera singers helped to elevate the phonograph from its status as a novelty or toy. After the sewing machine, the phonograph (Edison or Victrola) was the most complex mechanical device ever sold for home use.

Fred Gaisberg, a tireless and innovative worker in the recording studio, serves as a role model for the modern record producer. He was the pianist accompanying many of the early sessions. He also handled the recording artists themselves, stroking egos and soothing nerves when necessary. Recalling his early career, Gaisberg wrote of a common condition he called "Gramo-fright." Even the most stentorian operatic singers could be intimidated by the recording horn.

Victor's Red Seal classical catalogue, headed by Caruso and largely assembled by Gaisberg, was quickly established as a higher-priced status item; the other major companies, Edison and Columbia, had to play catch-up in developing their own musical stables.

Technology couldn't compensate for lackluster music choices. Columbia introduced a two-sided disc in 1904, retailing for $1.50. Four years later, Edison introduced a souped-up cylinder: the Amberol (featuring four-minute duration) and later, Blue Amberol. Composed of tough blue celluloid, the upgraded cylinder lasted longer and sounded better. "The sweet tone that has always marked Edison Amberol Records . . . will be enhanced by Blue Amberol." So read the ad copy, anyway.

Despite the highbrow hype, vaudeville and marching band titles outsold classical from the start. Fred Gaisberg, high-tech talent scout, toured Europe and recorded scores of classical virtuosos. Yet at home he (and his peers at the other companies) also recorded anything that would sell: dance music, ethnic specialties, folk songs, marches, sentimental ballads, hymns, coon songs, sermons, comic monologues, recitations, sound reenactments of historic events.

Still, the Red Seal label maintained the mark of class; these records cost more but they were indeed popular. Red Seal records made celebrities of the musicians, and the musicians made discs their medium. Caruso's voice was perfectly suited to the talking machine; he injected an ecstatic degree of palpable drama and emotion into his performances. His voice emerged from the horn with clarity and power, drowning out some of the surface noise.

Caruso's success marked the beginning of the celebrity cult or star system in the music business—a trend resisted by Thomas Edison, who preferred to see his own name and image emblazoned on his record releases. Despite Edison's wishes, recording artists were replacing inventors as the personalities associated with the phonograph. Enrico Caruso became synonymous with the Victrola; one phenomenon couldn't have become so popular without the other.

Half a century later, the Caruso of his time—a guy named Elvis Presley—toiled for the direct corporate descendant of the Victor Company, RCA Victor. In 1960, "It's Now or Never" became something more than the latest Elvis single to reach number one on the pop charts. Its lilting melody comes directly from "There's No Tomorrow" by Tony Martin. *That* song, a number one for Martin in 1949, simply retools the traditional Italian folk tune "O Sole Mio." Indeed, the singer who originally immortalized "O Sole Mio" on a 1916 Victor recording was Enrico Caruso. Completing the musical circle, Elvis always said he could remember listening to Caruso's records as a child.

## The First Dance Craze

Despite Caruso's success, the future of the phonograph rested in pop. Music hall ballads, Broadway show tunes, folk songs, ersatz ethnic ditties: the popular styles of the early twentieth century were perfectly suited to records owing to their brief duration. At any rate, they were easier to squeeze into the arbitrary three-minute format than an opera aria or symphony movement. Even popular songs had to be edited or shortened. The sound of military or marching band music was one of the first popular trends; John Philip Sousa and his Marine Band, exclusively signed to the fledgling Columbia label, were leaders in this field. Marching bands had been a live-performance mainstay of nineteenth-century culture, when every small town or neighborhood could assemble one at holiday time. The strident, brassy intonation of the marching bands easily lent itself to the limited range of the early recording horns.

As the century progressed, sound reproduction grew more sophisticated, and more phonographs and Victrolas were sold. The demand for recordings increased, and the amazing breadth of America's polyglot culture became apparent. African-American music, with its emphasis on syncopated rhythms and unbridled emotional expression, became the definitive sound of the new machine and the new era. Perhaps Andre Millard says it best in his landmark survey *America on Record*—"The single most important cultural accomplishment of the industry of recorded sound in the twentieth century was to make black U.S. music the popular music of the world."

Decades before Dick Clark and *American Bandstand*, the measure of a hit record was rhythm and movement. "It's got a good beat and you can dance to it." Syncopation seduced American ears and feet. Black music provided a break from staid Victorian conventions, the genteel heart songs and the tuneful deluge of Tin Pan Alley hackwork. Coon songs, with their crude stereotyping of black speech and culture, set the stage. Hokey, racially insensitive minstrel characters such as Jim Dandy and Jimmy-crack-corn-and-I-don't-care were already staples on the vaudeville circuit, having predated the recording era. Grossly offensive by current standards, these blackface routines—and their immense popularity on record—signal the hidden riches and twisted allure of black culture in America. African music mutated into something rich and mysterious in the New World: a buried treasure waiting to be plumbed by the nascent recording industry.

Records crossed racial and social boundaries from the start. Early spoken-word recordings satirized and celebrated the experience of recent immigrants; but their ethnic humor wasn't mutually exclusive. My late grandfather, a stereotypical first-generation Irish American born in 1893, could recite the Eastern-European spoof "Cohen at the Telephone" from memory; it received pride of placement alongside his favorite self-deprecating Paddy and Mike routines. He'd learned them all from records in his teens, and remembered them well into his seventies. The editor of *Phonoscope* magazine, Russell Hunting, recorded his prized recitation of "Cohen" in the 1890s. His cylinders became so popular that second-generation duplicates were made without his knowledge—an early example of pirate, or bootleg, recordings.

And at the turn of the last century, ragtime triggered a musical fad with lasting repercussions. Ragtime laid down the rhythms that would revolutionize popular tastes in America. Also known as barrelhouse, boogie, and honky-tonk, this syncopated piano sound created a pattern that would repeat throughout the next 100 years: A new style of black music inspires a new dance craze, and the phonograph (or record player or turntable) becomes its natural carrier. Technology is the prime mover behind pop music. Ragtime was not only black music, it was proudly self-identified black music. There could be no mistaking ragtime as a parody or appropriation; it was the real thing. Ragtime defined a rhythm and sound, representing an attitude and a social force. Ragtime ruled as did rock 'n' roll sixty years later.

Scott Joplin is rightly hailed as the champion and originator of ragtime; though the style was born in the saloons and brothels of big cities, he nailed it down. Joplin transcribed its serpentine beat onto paper, a Herculean feat. And it was Irving Berlin, a Jewish-American product of New York City's Lower East Side, who wrote the standard, "Alexander's Ragtime Band." Democracy in action: the lines of race and class get blurred once the records start spinning. "Syncopation," said Berlin, "is the soul of every true American."

The first recording of "Alexander's Ragtime Band," by the minstrel show duo Arthur Collins and Byron Harlan, helped to spread the new beat. Estimates are unreliable, but let's just say that Collins and Harlan sold *a lot* of discs and cylinders in the years before World War I. The comedy duo specialized in coon songs and dialect humor. "Bake Dat Chicken Pie" and "Alabama Jubilee" were balanced by "Down Where the Wurzburger Flows" and "Under the Anheuser Bush." Collins and Harlan were clever businessmen, as well as clowns. They'd latch onto a suitable musical vehicle such as "Alexander" and record subsequent versions for each of the Big Three record companies: Edison, Victor, Columbia. Next came the European Pathe label and smaller outfits such as Emerson. For years, it worked: Arthur Collins recorded his solo hit "The Preacher and the Bear" for six labels alone. (This venerable routine has been recorded as recently as 1970, when soul veteran Rufus Thomas added it to his string of comic R&B singles on the Stax label.) In retrospect, the reliable *Billboard* chart compiler Joel Whitburn reckons that "The Preacher and the Bear" by Arthur Collins became the "first generally recognized million seller" in 1905. Some suspect Len Spencer may have done it around 1902, with his "Arkansaw [*sic*] Traveller."

By the time they recorded "Darktown Strutters' Ball" in 1918, however, the appeal of Collins and Harlan had waned. They couldn't match the energy and strut of the Original Dixieland Jazz Band—white guys who didn't wear blackface, literally or figuratively. Faced by the Jazz Age, minstrels and coon songs finally began to fade by the 1920s.

While ragtime came from the dark side of the city, the blues crept out of the backcountry and seeped into the public consciousness around the same time. W. C. Handy published his "St. Louis Blues" in 1914; like Joplin with ragtime, Handy was the first to take the oral tradition of the blues, translate it into notation, and transcribe it on paper so it could be recorded. Soon the melancholy magic of the blues—moaning voices and slurred notes—popped up on the vaudeville circuit and on records.

By this time, records meant round objects with a hole in the middle: Twenty-three million discs were manufactured in 1914, as opposed to just three million cylinders. Edison stood fast by his format, almost alone. Consumers bought both 10- and 12-inch discs, often selecting the 10-inch records for popular and 12-inch for classical. Overall, the record business was booming. In 1914, there were eighteen companies in the business of recorded sound; by 1918, there were 166. During the same time frame, the value of the industry's products rose from $27 million in 1914 to $158 million in 1918. In 1914, Americans purchased half a million phonographs or talking machines, and twenty-seven million records.

## Edison: The Long Goodbye

In 1913, Edison caved. True, he continued making cylinders, but he felt compelled to bring out a disc phonograph. Columbia discontinued cylinders in 1912. As the sales of Victor discs soared, the Edison cylinders were demoted to office dictation, their original purpose. The Edison Disc Phonograph was a high-end item. It wasn't a rousing success.

The Edison Diamond Discs took their name from the pointed tip of the phonograph's stylus. The diamond needles never needed to be replaced, or so said the ad copy. According to owners, the metal needle on Victor or Columbia machines had to go after two plays or they'd start to scratch the record. On the downside, Edison Diamond Discs were 10 inches wide and weighed 10 ounces; the top-of-the-line Victor records measured 12 inches wide and weighed just 8 ounces. Diamond discs needed to be heavy to withstand the steady pressure of that big needle riding in the grooves.

Edison wielded an intuitive, seat-of-his-pants understanding of the physics of music. This may have blinded him to certain limitations. Take the so-called hill and dale method Edison relied on—vertical modulation—to cut the grooves in his recordings; Berliner used lateral modulation. This arcane terminology refers to the way the sound waves are carved or etched into the individual grooves on the recording surface. The cut of the groove shapes the path of the stylus. On vertically cut records, the stylus moved up (hill) and down (dale); on laterally cut records, it moved side to side. Vertical modulation seemed to work well on Edison cylinders, but some people thought the hill and dale–style discs were extra vulnerable to distortion and noise. And the Edison Disc Phonograph's cabinet was "deemed less attractive than the Victrola" by Edison himself. Even more unattractive, those vertical-cut discs were incompatible with other disc phonographs.

Edison made at least one mistake that doesn't come as a surprise. In his wisdom, he decided that Edison Diamond Discs would not carry the artists' names on the disc itself. The record sleeve contained that vital information, though you couldn't always read it.

Beginning in 1913, Edison introduced his disc phonograph with a series of "Edison Tone-Test Recitals." These contests matched phonograph against a live singer in (virtual) blindfold comparison for the audience. Underneath the bravado, we can sense the scope and urgency of Edison's mission. Discs (or cylinders) should recreate musical performance, not merely record them. As he wrote in "Edison's Dream of New Music" (*Cosmopolitan*, May 1913),

> I shall yet put before the world a phonograph that will render whole operas better than the singers themselves could sing them in a theater. I shall do this by virtue of the fact that with a phonograph I can record the voices better than any person in a theater can hear them.

Unfortunately, Edison failed to follow up the tone-test publicity. A paucity of advertising further hampered the Diamond Disc campaign.

## Cakewalk and Kangaroo Dip

Classical music retained a small, devoted following, but for the most part, record consumers were not inclined to sit still while they listened. Blues and ragtime triggered a dance mania in America; this first bout of boogie fever lasted roughly from 1911 to 1917. African-American folk dances started showing up in society balls: the cakewalk, bunny hug, turkey trot, grizzly bear, monkey glide, kangaroo dip. Based on animal movements, as the names suggest, these steps made room for individual variation and improvisation. Naturally, their reliance on movements originating from the pelvic region (thrust) and physical contact between partners ("neck holding") scandalized the moral guardians of the period. Even in socially acceptable, somewhat softened form, these new rhythms and dances jostled the social order and jump-started a pop tradition. Jazz, swing, R&B, rock 'n' roll, soul, disco, hiphop, techno, you name it: the bodies and the turntables still go round and round.

Vernon and Irene Castle ruled as the original king and queen of dance crossover: the cakewalk's upper-crust ambassadors. They civilized black dance steps, transporting the funky strut to society ballrooms and, via their best-selling recordings, middle-class living rooms. Some would compare their influence to that of Pat Boone's whitened and lightened R&B cover versions. But the Castles didn't just benefit from ragtime and the blues, they helped promote and spread the word. They may have smoothed over some of the earthy origins of their grooves, but not entirely. Black musicians usually backed them. The dance craze of the teens called for special accompaniment, and dance bands and dance records soon filled the air with syncopated sounds. Of course, an older generation (and "serious" music lovers) considered all this a threat to the social order and called it noise. That started another venerable pop tradition.

The Castles' secret weapon was a Harlem-based bandleader named James Reese Europe. His smooth arrangements and syncopated beat, achieved with unusual instrumentation, captivated the dancing couple at a swank Manhattan party. The Castles teamed up with Europe, performing with his Exclusive Society Orchestra around the country. The musicians also found work at the Castle House, Vernon and Irene's dance school. Previously,

Europe had organized the Clef Club, an informal union and booking agency for local black musicians. In 1912, he played New York's prestigious Carnegie Hall with a group of Clef Club players. At the time, Clef's working band lineup might include banjo, mandolin, violin, clarinet, cornet, and drums.

The first dance craze demanded specialized accompaniment, small groups such as Europe's who could play syncopated riffs. It sounded easier than it was. Though accompaniments at dance halls and performances were usually live, dance mania fueled rather than impeded phonograph and record sales. These smaller groups, with their percussive melodies and pronounced beat, were tailor-made for the primitive recording studio. In fact, their syncopated sound was more easily duplicated by phonograph than by local musicians. A volatile substance, ragtime changed as it grew in popularity. By the late teens, the sound had morphed into something eventually called jazz. Louder, looser, more improvised and more exciting than ragtime, jazz brought drums and percussion to the fore. The instrumental emphasis switched from solo piano to saxophone and trumpet breaks, played with "hot" flashes of sexual urgency. And yes, you could still dance to it.

# chapter 2

# WAR ON CANNED MUSIC

JAZZ AND ITS COUNTRY COUSIN, the blues, continued the dance boom after World War I. Reaching its peak during the late twenties, the jazz and blues craze coincided with the adolescent phase of the record industry.

Pressure from another growing technology put the phonograph to its first external test. The rise of radio nearly submerged the record player. In the second half of the 1920s, electrical recording salvaged the situation with vastly improved sound quality. Microphones and amplifiers replaced horns and recording phonographs; the job description for a musician profoundly changed as a result. The purpose of making records shifted away from audio documentation and moved toward aural creation.

The increased volume and heavy bass provided by radio's electronic amplification—as opposed to the speaker horns of early phonographs—was perfectly suited to pop tastes of the period. Radios were smartly marketed as pieces of furniture in a variety of styles, a fine addition to any living room. Phonographs, especially the ever-popular Victrola, were utilitarian by comparison. The Christmas shopping season of 1924 signaled a showdown between the fledgling home entertainment systems, and phono-graphs came up short. In the following year, the once-booming Victor Talking Machine Company lost $6.5 million. (Tellingly, the Radio Corporation of America would buy Victor in 1929.) As much as the music, the *sound* of radio—loud, clear, smooth, bass heavy, not "tinny"—became the next craze.

Then came 1929. Another economic boom bites the dust. The Great Depression set the scene for the second format war.

Through thick and thin, music technology served as America's engine of cultural integration, decades before the civil rights movement. In the days before the advent of commercial radio, a blues singer named Mamie Smith inaugurated the pop tradition of crossover. Her 1920 recording "Crazy Blues" caught fire with a broad audience. Cut for the tiny Okeh label, "Crazy Blues" by Mamie Smith and her Jazz Hounds appealed to black and white listeners alike. This catchy twelve-bar plaint sold more than 70,000 copies, paving the way for the blues stars Ma Rainey, Bessie Smith, Ida Cox, and Alberta Hunter. Smith's "Crazy Blues" session employed all black musicians, another significant precedent. The first black blues singer to be commercially recorded, Smith was recruited and recorded by talent scout Ralph Peer. He was a pioneer, too. Peer identified the markets for "race" and "hillbilly" music, and coined those terms for the record industry.

Some things remained the same. Later in 1920, the Original Dixieland Jazz Band enjoyed equal or better success with an in-strumental reading of "Crazy Blues." The white group's version benefited (if that's the word) from a kazoo solo. The jazz and blues fad fueled and funded a wave of independent record com-panies in the twenties: Black Swan, Brunswick, Paramount, Vocalion, and dozens more. Despite their broad-based appeal, releases from these labels were largely absent from the airwaves. Images of F. Scott Fitzgerald, flappers, and flaming youth cloud the rearview mirror. In musical terms, the Jazz Age was more a cultural phenomenon than a commercial revolution. Bear in mind, however, that most blues recordings of the 1920s represented urbanized versions of the southern backwoods sound—not folk music, but pop records. The acoustic blues of the Mississippi Delta begins its crossover journey decades later.

Jazz was urbanized music by definition: born in New Orleans, exported to Chicago when Kid Ory and Louis Armstrong hopped a northbound train. Just like Enrico Caruso twenty years earlier, Armstrong was a "natural" in the studio. Their performances didn't have to be adjusted or adapted to technology; amplifier and microphone magically captured their full effect. The electrical recording process played to Armstrong's strengths. The melodic exuberance of his trumpet solos advertised the expanded dynamic range of the new technology. Powered by snappy syncopation, driven by percussive beats, Louis Armstrong's virtuosity flows in up-tempo three-minute bursts. "West End Blues" makes you want to move when heard in anachronistic CD crystal clarity; back in the day, jazz records were dance records by definition. On the dance floor, the Charleston ruled over all. Among the smart set, the earthy, grinding black bottom was all the rage.

The pop crossover phenomenon, however, wasn't always a two-way street. The initial success of the blues legend Bessie Smith signals the underlying reality of segregation. Her "Down Hearted Blues" sold more than a million copies in 1923, purchased by a largely black audience. The so-called race market offered a robust and lucrative niche for the record companies—and so begins another venerable tradition.

Yet Ralph Peer's early "hillbilly" discoveries such as Fiddlin' John Carson and Vernon Dalhart were regional successes limited to white audiences. Born in Texas, Marion Try Slaughter improbably developed an interest in opera singing. He moved east and became a trained tenor. He assumed his professional name by merging two adjacent towns (Vernon and Dalhart) of his native Texas. In 1916, he focused his vocal talents on truly esoteric fare, commercialized folk music. Following the time-honored tradition, Dalhart serially recorded "The Prisoner's Song." Nearly one million copies shipped in 1925 alone, yet Dalhart remained mostly unknown—and unheard—in the major cities. Ultimately, he cut close to thirty versions for more than ten labels, including Victor and the fading Edison. In fact, Dalhart remained loyal to Edison through the 1920s—he hit the road for some public tone-test demonstrations. The opera snob inventor originally signed Dalhart as a classical artist, of course; yet he gladly released Dalhart's hillbilly discs and cylinders right up to 1929, when he closed shop. Dalhart wisely followed his nationwide success with a reworked traditional. His hit rendition of "The Wreck of the Old '97" along with "The Prisoner's Song" laid the foundation of the modern country music business. Other record and phonograph companies quickly woke up and fed the new hillbilly market. Vernon Dalhart had spawned an ungainly youth with a healthy appetite.

In 1926, *Variety* sketched out a scenario for its inside-dopester show business audience by proclaiming, "The talking machine to the hillbilly is more practical than his bible." Special note was taken of the rubes' penchant for purchasing successive copies of a single song—six or more. They literally played the records until they wore them out. Of course, a handful of plays with a cheap stylus could demolish the grooves on any disc; still, it was a marketer's dream. Hillbilly music—later country and western—permanently settled into a profitable niche in the pop marketplace.

## The Rise of Radio

> The phonograph opens the cramped urban cell into as many worlds as there are records . . . radio makes the whole world a domestic scene.
> —Evan Eisenberg, *The Recording Angel*

Thanks to its vacuum tubes and amplified speakers, radio was a sonic revelation for listeners. Music on radio sounded better than on a phonograph. And once you owned a radio, it didn't cost a thing.

KDKA, in Pittsburgh, Pennsylvania, sent forth the first commercial radio broadcast, announcing the election of Warren G. Harding as President of the United States. The date was November 6, 1920. Owned by Westinghouse Electric, KDKA was actually conceived in amateur broadcasts around the Pittsburgh area. A Westinghouse engineer named Frank Conrad assembled a crude transmitter and hit the airwaves: playing records was his specialty, and he attracted plenty of attention. A local department store sold radio receivers specifically for accessing Conrad's show. After that, Westinghouse higher-ups latched onto the idea in a hurry. It didn't take long to realize that radio *stations* can help sell radios.

In New York City, a little more than one year later, the first paid radio commercial aired on WEAF. (Owned by American Telephone & Telegraph, this station later became WNBC.) The Radio Corporation of America, better known as RCA, had been formed in 1919. Using World War I as an excuse, the U.S. government had taken control of 6,000 existing radio stations in 1916. They were either turned over to the navy for the duration or shuttered outright. And their patents too were appropriated, so experimentation also ground to a halt until the war ended two years later. After that, the government worked to support the RCA venture by relaxing antitrust objections. Also aligned in RCA's support were the corporate heavy hitters of the day. General Electric, Westinghouse, AT&T, and United Fruit all handed over patents as a form of investment, with the result that the British-owned American Marconi Company stepped out of the peacetime radio scene soon after.

By winter 1922, a definite chill was felt in the phonograph business. That same year, the Department of Commerce set an aggressive precedent. Broadcast licenses were granted only to stations that promised *not* to play records. Practically speaking, however, most stations never really stopped playing them.

## The Sound of Electricity

After 1924, the formative phase of the phonograph—the acoustic era—quickly passed into history. Behind the scenes, the phonograph industry played catch-up while radio still ruled. The big three companies—Victor, Columbia, and Edison—gradually adapted *electrical recording* technology. H. C. Harrison, an engineer employed by Western Electric, captured the patent in May 1924. This marked a major breakthrough. Just a few months later, however, the commercial phonograph industry stumbled into a major slump.

By the 1920s, Thomas Edison was a sideshow; he catered to specialists and the so-called carriage trade. His Diamond Discs were considered technically perfect, though Edison's highfalutin taste in music—mostly classical—severely limited his commercial impact on the Jazz Age. He was also the last of the big three to "go electric."

One gigantic disadvantage of acoustic phonographs was volume control. There wasn't any. The vacuum tubes in radios received broadcast signals and amplified them through dynamic speakers, translating sound waves into electrical currents, like the telephone. Crude in comparison, acoustic phonographs transcribed the shape and pattern of sound waves directly into discs for playback through a horn.

Dynamic speakers liberated radio listeners from earphones. You could not only annoy your neighbors, you could also control the din. And that was a definite advantage over the old speaker horns. While radio's amplified sound permitted loudness to be raised and lowered, the volume of acoustic phonographs could only be dampened. The Victrola's cabinet featured doors that could be opened or shut in front of the speaker horn; the Edison Diamond Disc player achieved this effect with a ball of soft cloth that fit into the speaker horn, hence the expression *put a sock in it*.

By the time Mamie Smith returned to Columbia's New York studio in 1925, a Western Electric microphone instead of the old-fashioned recording horn confronted her. Musicians no longer needed to position themselves around the horn since the dynamics of a large orchestra wouldn't jostle the recording needle. Instruments that were inaudible in the acoustic recording era—drum, violin, bass—would now register loud and clear.

In 1925, Victor introduced the Othophonic Victrola—an acoustic machine that played electrically recorded discs—and quickly rebounded from its sales slump. The tone of the Othophonic Victrola was billed as "radio timbre." One year later, Victor pulled in an estimated $7 million profit. Also in 1925, Brunswick brought out the first all-electric machine, the Panatrope, with dynamic loudspeakers and magnetic stylus. A year later, Columbia tested the waters with its electric Vitaphone. Two years later, Victor debuted a phonograph with a record changer. Edison tentatively unveiled a forty-minute long-playing disc. A new era was under way, but the phonograph industry wasn't out of the woods yet.

For all their impact on the zeitgeist, hopping jazz records were never as popular with the mainstream as sentimental ballads and sweet, slow, band instrumentals. Sometimes technological milestones are marked by novelty hits. The success of "Whispering" Jack Smith, for instance, neatly demonstrated the transforming power of the microphone; his breathy speak-sing delivery—the result of a World War I injury—wouldn't have flown without the propelling force of electric amplification. Microphones could turn even a timid voice into a vocal presence. Also in the late 1920s, Rudy Vallée gained fame by purring into a megaphone. Utterly dependent on then crude technology, he made that crutch his gimmick.

In the case of blues and jazz, recording imposed structure and discipline—three minutes' worth anyway—on a semi-improvised approach to playing. The loss of energy and spontaneity must be mourned, but electrically recorded discs captured something new as well: the musicians' audible sense of freedom, all their twists and turns and quirks and flourishes. Now the stuff that couldn't be written down—the aura or underlying vibe—was preserved forever in crackling black plastic.

## Edison: The End

Ironically, by the 1920s, deafness was the defining force behind Edison's decisions in the phonograph business. His musical taste—always suspect—was now grossly distorted by hearing problems. Many singers who auditioned for Edison got the thumbs-down, professionals and amateurs alike. They all sounded shrill and painful to his ears, drenched in tremolo and stinging vibrato. Stubbornly, he always insisted the problem was with the singers. With its meticulous accuracy and bell-like clarity, the Edison phonograph indeed magnified any singer's shortcomings.

When his sons suggested that he branch into radio mid-decade, for the first time Edison hesitated and got left behind. When he finally delivered a combination radio-phonograph in 1928, it was too late. Thomas Edison, self-styled patriarch of the recording industry, discontinued record and phonograph production one year later. It happened soon after the 1929 stock market crash, but Edison's fate was already sealed. By 1930, Edison discontinued his struggling radio operation and began winding down his career; he deserved a rest. But at that point, the future of the phonograph itself was in grave doubt.

## Radio Versus Records

The killer competition between radio and records had settled into a symbiotic relationship by the time the stock market crashed in 1929. All those shiny new Othophonics, Panatones, and Vitaphones were spinning discs, and many of them were recordings by radio stars. Both mediums suffered during the ensuing Depression, but the phonograph industry was hit harder. After all, radio was still free.

The manufacture of record players had all but ceased by 1930. Disc sales had dropped by half. Record sales hit 110 million in 1922; ten years later, the figure had fallen to six million. Phonographs and records were no longer advertised. Radio suffered, since many stations secretly relied on recorded music, which infuriated recording musicians and their unions. The decline in disc sales ultimately meant fewer records to choose from, and the broadcast selection had always been spotty. All of a sudden, it got worse: you heard the same popular song nine or ten times a day. Repetition ruled the airwaves. By 1932, the U.S. music industry touched rock bottom.

The use of records on the radio turned into a major battle during the format wars. But radio's reliance on live performers ultimately petered out for economic reasons as well as technological and musical ones. In the end, it was always cheaper to play recorded music than pay and maintain live musicians.

With their studio orchestras and musical guest stars, the major radio networks (NBC, CBS, and Mutual) created a national standard of entertainment: in effect, they raised the bar on musicianship. Audiences came to expect more because they'd heard the best big bands and pop vocalists (especially Bing Crosby) on a regular basis. Suddenly, the local dance band sawing away on the hits of the day, a staple of most radio stations, didn't sound so good. They didn't sound like records on the phonograph.

In 1926, the National Broadcasting Company debuted with a twenty-four-station radio network. (NBC was backed by RCA.) One year later, Columbia Phonograph bought United Independent Network, and the independent Columbia Broadcasting System (CBS) was born. At the same time, the U.S. bureaucracy—in the form of the Federal Radio Commission, precursor of the Federal Communications Commission—reared its head for the first time. Broadcasting endured much government regulation from here on.

The NBC and CBS radio networks actually banned record playing in 1930, under pressure from Tin Pan Alley music publishers and the new pugnacious musicians union. By all accounts, the ban was selectively enforced at best, so many stations kept on spinning. The networks incorporated records in their programming only gradually, grudgingly. Behind the scenes, however, the very concept of a radio network quietly came to depend on discs. Custom-made records—transcription discs—provided a crucial technological fix in the transmission of live programs on radio.

Invented by the Vitaphone Company's Harold C. Smith, transcription discs were oversize (16 inch), slow turning (33$^1/_3$ rpm), and long (fifteen minutes per side). The discs were originally intended for the film industry, but they lent themselves to the role of transcribing (recording) and storing content for future broadcast. These bulky platters carried music, drama, comedy, and advertisements. Often spaces were left silent for local advertising inserts. Transcription discs could be used all along the network, courtesy of the U.S. mail. Time zone problems and scheduling difficulties could be easily averted.

Just a couple of years after their introduction, in 1932, transcription discs were used on 75 percent of all radio stations. By 1939, many smaller stations relied on these prerecorded broadcasts for the bulk of their programming. Network radio could effectively ban record playing, but they needed record technology in order to broadcast "live" music. Despite the efforts of the musicians union, record technology thoroughly infiltrated radio.

## "Canned Music"

Enter the dragon. James Caesar Petrillo acted as an open foe of records and recording. He crusaded for the musicians union. He was a man on a mission, leading a twenty-year campaign against the record and phonograph (later jukebox) industry. Rising in the 1930s, Petrillo distinguished himself as a media-savvy master: he wielded lawsuits and press releases with equal aplomb. Eventually, he was elected national president of the American Federation of Musicians.

In Joseph P. Kraft's labor history *From Stage to Studio*, Petrillo emerges as a compelling leader and complex human being. He's not so easy to dismiss as either Luddite or publicity hound. "Disaffected musicians did not stand passively by while the revolution capsized their lives," writes Kraft. "On the contrary, in myriad and clever ways, and largely through their union, they sought to control the forces of change."

Petrillo first caught the public eye in Chicago, where he served as the firebrand president of the musicians' local. In 1927, he denounced local radio stations for the heinous crime of playing records. One of the stations he sued, WCRW, was owned and operated by Clinton R. White, who was also an old-school inventor; all the discs aired on WCRW spun on White's own patented turntable, the vibraphone.

By 1928, Petrillo regularly hurled thunderbolts at the phonograph and radio interests. At one point, he considered "waging open war against mechanical devices in general." He branded records with the derogatory description *canned music*, and endless repetition made it stick. Petrillo was persistent and ingenious. Perhaps his most infamous and lasting action occurred in 1929, when he issued an ultimatum that affected all Chicago radio stations. The requirement was simple. If you use a record player in your studios, then you must hire a union musician to operate the turntables. Before the disc jockey, stations were compelled to acquire a flunky: the lowly pancake turner. His job was a joke. This borderline-corrupt practice persisted for more than a decade.

Petrillo saw himself, of course, as champion of the working stiff. In his own defense, he'd invoke his noble quest for musicians' basic right to employment. The use of "canned music" cost lots of musicians their jobs, no question about it. Looking back, Petrillo's zeal seems understandable, though severely misguided. He tried to protect musicians and shield them from the impact of recording technology, but by doing so he ensured their ultimate replacement by machines. Perhaps he could have served them better by helping them absorb the change, but in any case, his reactionary campaign was finally repelled after a protracted fight.

In 1933, Petrillo and the AFM asked for a ban on all broadcasts of recordings. He didn't get it, but he wasn't about to go away.

## Jukebox Music

The fate of the phonograph ultimately was determined by a hungry public eager for music, just as it had been in the 1890s. Just because people couldn't afford record players or records didn't mean they were tired of listening—or dancing. A coin-op machine came to the rescue.

The jukebox transported the phonograph to public space and bested radio by featuring *choices*. On radio, selection is always made for the listener. Listeners may choose who selects by changing stations; you can't select the songs, but you can switch formats.

In the days of the penny arcade, the mass appeal of the original coin-op amusements was sheer novelty, the miracle of hearing recorded music, and the penny-pleasure machines soon became widespread. In 1888, Thomas Adams installed the first Tutti Frutti confection dispenser in a New York train station. Even the great Lieutenant Bettini tested the coin-op field when his opera activities waned; the wannabe inventor obtained a patent for his own gumball machine in 1914. While he may have been eccentric, he was nobody's fool. All those pennies and nickels frittered away for the sake of amusement eventually add up, and without question this contributed to the survival of the phonograph.

By the 1920s, mechanical instruments—namely, the player piano—dominated the field of automated music. Attempts at making a coin-op phonograph yielded impractical and sometimes comic results. Mills Novelty Company of Chicago concocted a somewhat convoluted solution. Their machine was called the Dance Master, a jukebox prototype that offered twelve selections—and used twelve turntables rotating like a Ferris wheel.

Practically speaking, the first coin-slot machine with electric amplification and a multirecord changer was built by American Music Industries (AMI) in 1927. The Wurlitzer, Seeburg, and Rockola Companies all followed suit. Outside of movie theaters, *jukeboxes*, as they came to be known, delivered the best sound reproduction available at the time. Since jukeboxes were often situated in bars and restaurants, the repeal of Prohibition in 1933 greatly enhanced their appeal. Loud music for dancing and suggestive novelties fared best on the new machines. The rise of hillbilly and race records in the 1920s continued apace in jukeboxes in the 1930s: the hillbilly market tripled during the years 1930–1932 alone. Half of all records produced in 1936 were destined for jukeboxes, and half of these machines were in the South. By 1939, 225,000 jukeboxes consumed thirteen million discs per year.

The jukebox success story springs from two sources. One is that unique feature of the phonograph that is selection, or user choice. Swing is the second reason. Those syncopated rhythms sucked up a lot of jukebox nickels.

The advent of swing—danceable big-band jazz—started on jukeboxes and gradually spread to a new generation of home phonographs. In general, jukeboxes pushed swing to young people while radio provided classical music for their parents. Eventually, the record industry found an economic way to serve these evolving tastes.

Victor, now aligned with RCA, made the most of its new position. Victor's Duo Jr., introduced in 1934, was simple genius: an electrically powered phonograph that attached to a radio set. Priced at a reasonable $16.50, the Duo Jr. consisted of a turntable, cartridge, and tonearm tucked away in a plastic case. The Duo Jr.

caught on just as Columbia's similar radiograph attachment (overpriced at $55) did not.

Similarly, a move to discount the price of pop records jump-started the swing phenomenon. Jack Kapp of the British-owned Decca Company dropped the price of 10-inch 78 rpm dance records from 75¢ to 35¢.

There were other, competing budget labels at the time: Columbia now owned Okeh (and later Brunswick). Victor had its Bluebird (25¢) line. Decca was different, because its budget line offered first-tier "name" artists such as Bing Crosby, the Dorsey Brothers, Guy Lombardo, the Mills Brothers, and Fletcher Henderson's big band. Kapp also insisted on high-quality discs for the budget line—anything to compete with radio.

Thanks to electrical recording and amplification, smooth-voiced male singers came across more effectively on record than they ever had in the acoustic era. The trend began with megaphone-enhanced Rudy Vallée. Soon the crooning style dominated American pop vocals, no small thanks to the *uber*confident recordings of Bing Crosby and Frank Sinatra. A new generation of youth adopted these sounds, embracing the singers of big bands as idols. As World War II loomed, popular music began to wield a bewitching power over young Americans that even movies couldn't match.

## Dancing Machine

When I joined Fred Waring [in 1937] he was anti-recording. He had a whole scene going with [Paul] Whiteman, the Dorsey Brothers, Benny Goodman, to ban recording.

Fred was the leader of it. And he had musicians signing
up, pledging not to make a phonograph record.

—Les Paul

As the popularity of the jukebox helped revive the record business, there was, of course, organized resistance from the AFM,
not to mention a propaganda campaign. Petrillo cashed in some
of his chits with prominent musicians. Bandleader Fred Waring
emerged as the official AFM spokesman; as well as handling public relations, he proselytized for the recording ban. The conductor
of a pop choir called the Pennsylvanians, Waring was known for
his radio "glee club" programs. His recording career didn't suffer
because of his AFM support, it ceased to exist. Waring backed up
his protest with deeds: he actually quit making records for more
than a decade, starting in 1932. Reportedly, Waring also promoted the recording ban efforts by donating a hefty sum of his
own money.

Arguments among working musicians revolved around the art
of hype, or overplugging. Their fear was overzealous marketing,
too much hard sell on too few records. Unfortunately, there was a
deeper problem: music quality lagged behind the improved technology. Most of the secondhand Tin Pan Alley material flooding
the thirties pop market was a washout. Swing was the new craze.
Swing didn't start to really move records (and record players) until
about 1937. Melody, not rhythm, ruled the radio.

Petrillo and the AFM openly longed for an equivalent to the
(relatively small) radio royalty received by the American Society
of Composers, Authors and Publishers (ASCAP). Established in
1914, ASCAP protected the copyright interests of songwriters and

publishers, the connected denizens of New York's famed Tin Pan Alley. ASCAP had claimed a piece of the radio pie in 1922, but its share fell off during the Depression.

Predictably, ASCAP turned a deaf ear to the jukebox music explosion in the thirties. That's when Broadcast Music International (BMI) stepped in. Formed in 1939, BMI emerged as ASCAP's eager sibling, younger and hungrier. BMI existed to service the needs of local radio stations and at the same time promote regional music. BMI also lifted the bar on song publishing: the list opened up to small-label performers—that is, "hillbilly" and black—who'd been excluded by ASCAP.

With Petrilloesque defiance, ASCAP overplayed its hand during a radio royalty dispute. After two years of tense negotiations, ASCAP finally pulled its songs from the radio. This strike lasted ten long months in 1941, but ASCAP's supposed show of strength wound up crippling the venerable publishers' group in the long run. ASCAP was forced to settle with the radio networks for a lower royalty rate. Meanwhile, in the absence of any ASCAP songs on the air, BMI had picked up the slack.

By the tail end of the 1930s, recorded sound was on the rebound. Loudspeaker research conducted by the film industry (in order to fill giant theaters with sound) was positively affecting the phonograph field. Record players became smaller and more efficient; records sounded better and lasted longer. Shellac, the main ingredient in records, became extremely limited due to wartime shortages and would eventually be replaced by vinyl, which was lighter, more durable, and less expensive. But as the physical material for recordings temporarily dried up with the onset of World War II, so did America's musical resources.

After years of threats, in 1942 the impossible happened. James Petrillo and American Federation of Musicians went on strike, and recording virtually stopped for more than a year. The dispute, over royalties, was eventually settled to the satisfaction of AFM's tenacious leader. But Petrillo's long-range dreams were doomed: financial restitution for jobs sacrificed to technology is a lost cause. The postwar AFM recording boycott (in 1948) now seemed a Pyrrhic victory at best. For most working musicians, some sort of collaboration with technology was the only available means of survival.

In 1942, while Petrillo raged, the FCC conducted a study and concluded that music filled the airwaves three-quarters of the time overall. At the same time, nearly half of all U.S. radio stations exclusively relied on music for their programming needs.

Then the impossible happened again. Record sales were healthy in 1943, despite the shortage of material (shellac) and labor (musicians). The industry stockpiled just enough records to maintain the flow and stoke the fierce wartime need for entertainment. Further diversion was provided by a danceable new sound, complete with salty, sexy lyrics. Jukebox music increasingly made itself known on the radio and pop charts.

Al Dexter, born Clarence Albert Poindexter, recorded a so-called hillbilly novelty song called "Pistol Packin' Mama" in 1942. Falling between World War II and the AFM ban, his shot at the top of the pops looks like a textbook case of bad timing, yet once again, appearances deceive. A supple tune and a swaying beat made "Pistol Packin' Mama" the first country record to reach number one on the charts. Dexter's humorous plaint sold more than one million copies for the Okeh label. (Bing Crosby covered

"Mama" and walked away with his own million-seller on Decca.) Dexter was an exponent of the western swing sound, a hip-swaying mix of hillbilly twang and virtuoso jazz rhythm. He freely admitted to borrowing from western swing icon Bob Wills; in fact, "Pistol Packin' Mama" bears a close, almost fraternal resemblance to Wills's "Take Me Back to Tulsa." More important, Dexter had also fronted an all-black band at one point, because they were the best musicians available to him.

Improbably, a young record company arose in the midst of format war and confusion. Capitol Records, formed by the songwriter Johnny Mercer and others, established a beachhead during the wartime blitz. From the start, country- and blues-flavored material sustained the Hollywood-based label. "Cow Cow Boogie" by the singer Ella Mae Morse and pianist Freddie Slack—Capitol 102, its second release—climbed to the pop Top Ten in 1942. The funky aura of the roadhouse and honky-tonk rattled the decorum of Tin Pan Alley. Left-field flashes of brilliance such as "Cow Cow Boogie" and "Pistol Packin' Mama" illuminated the path toward a fresh music future. In the meantime, the world went to war and even records became part of the American campaign.

Victory Disc Records, manufacturer of V-discs, was a government-created company that existed for seven years in the 1940s. All told, Victory Disc issued around 900 of the 12-inch 78 rpm V-discs, and more than 2,700 songs were released in this format. Every style was represented: Louis Armstrong and Benny Goodman, Bing Crosby and Frank Sinatra, Ella Fitzgerald and Billie Holiday, the combined big bands of Jimmy and Tommy Dorsey, Arturo Toscanini conducting the NBC Symphony Orchestra. Even the musicians union and its strike on recording couldn't impede the war effort. Petrillo lifted the ban and let his union's members record V-discs—just as long as they weren't released commercially. For this reason, few V-discs survived. Petrillo had insisted that the discs be confiscated and destroyed after the war. He never backed down.

## chapter 3

# LOW ROAD TO HIGH FIDELITY

ONE AUTUMN NIGHT IN 1945, a dinner party is winding down in Westport, Connecticut. We're eavesdropping at the home of Mack and Helen Morgan. Musical accompaniment is Brahms's Second Piano Concerto. Vladimir Horowitz tickles the ivories, while Arturo Toscanini swings the baton. The only problem is that one of the Morgans' guests (and good friend) happens to be Dr. Peter Goldmark.

> In the midst of listening to the first movement of this record, a terrible thing happened. There was a click, silence, and strange noises and then the movement continued. This happened again and again. I counted twelve sides for the four movements and eleven interruptions, of which eight were unplanned by Brahms. So eight abominable times during the rendition I was in turn enthralled and jarred, like having the phone ring at intervals while you are making love. Gritting my teeth, I asked my friends to play the concerto a second time only to relive the horror.

My initial interest in the LP arose out of my sincere hatred of the phonograph. I am sure Thomas Edison never thought of it just this way, but to me the phonograph was a machine that learned how to talk but never learned how to make music.

Turning his attention to any engineering problem, Goldmark employed the "systems" approach: a complex relationship is always viewed as a whole. If one element changes, then everything else must change in order to maintain the overall integrity of the system. "In the case of the LP I proposed to change a number of things: amplifier, record material, shape of the groove, cartridge and stylus, method of recording, the turntable drive and, I remotely hoped, the musical taste of the nation."

Speed was not the only determining factor in perfecting the long-playing record. Needed to control and coordinate a combination of forces were wavelength of sound on record, cause of distortion, speed of record, and length of playing time. The length or duration of a record depends on three factors: disc diameter, rpm, and the number of grooves per inch in the area traversed by the needle. Writing in his autobiography *Maverick Inventor*, Goldmark implies that rpm is purely arbitrary. According to his study, 90 percent of all classical works would fit into forty-five minutes of playing time on a record, and 12 inches looked like an eminently practical size, considering that it fit all the turntables of the time.

First of all, to provide more playing time, it was necessary to change the number of grooves—which then necessitated changing the speed, which, in turn, required offsetting the limitation of frequency response which would have occurred. But we wanted just the opposite: a record with better frequency response, less distortion, and less noise.

When Goldmark presented his LP project to the president of Columbia Records, Ed Wallerstein, he was politely told to stick to television. Ever industrious, Goldmark was busy developing a color TV simultaneously with his record work. Wallerstein's condescending remark touched off the chief engineer's "Hungarian single-mindedness." He'd show this corporate lackey *exactly* what his CBS labs were capable of doing. Logically enough, those bulky radio transcription discs made a good starting point from which to build a long-playing record.

The styli available were maybe cactus, or something else reasonably sharp. So we had to miniaturize the groove in order to avoid distortion, because when you slow a record down, that means the linear speed toward the inside of the record would have created unbearable distortion. So we had to change the radius of the stylus. We went from sapphire to diamond. But in order for the tiny radii not to chew up the record, we had to reduce the pressure . . . but then the stylus wouldn't stay in the groove. So we had to introduce the old concept of compliance, which meant that the stylus had to have a certain vertical elasticity.

In other words, we had to develop a whole new science . . . we had to design new motors and drives, new pick up arm . . . we really had to tackle everything. Even microphones. So much was hidden in the shellac. People didn't realize why the record was noisy. So what we had to do was come up with a new material.

In those days vinyl was used experimentally for records, but it wasn't good enough, because the vinyl was expensive. But when we decided that you could put the whole [musical] work on a single record, then the cost of extra vinyl would be more or less offset. To use less vinyl we had to make the records thinner. But when the records were made thinner, you had trouble with warping and you had to find ways of stabilizing the vinyl, and that means different kinds of pressures.

Then you had a wonderful sound quality, but you didn't have a microphone capable of creating wonderful sounds. We found that the microphones were unable to reproduce what we called the buzz of the violin. So we started a whole study in microphones—using pistol shots to create sharp sound waves. We had to discover how to develop a new microphone, which turned out to be the condenser microphone. We found out what the Germans had already invented.

Then we turned to the loudspeaker, and had to develop an instrument. I'm not sure it's known, but we came up with the first so-called table hi-fi equipment; it was called a 360. We had to show that you didn't need a tremendous instrument to produce outstanding quality. So we found out how you can produce loud speakers and good low frequencies in a small enclosure by air venting and elastic suspension—out of which came the hi-fi industry.

When it finally emerged from the labs, CBS held a company-wide contest to name the new recording format. The entries narrowed down to a short list of twenty-five, all rejected. After that, Goldmark named his own invention, by accident. Offhandedly, he spoke the acronym for long player, LP, in the presence of Columbia Records' president. "That's it!" shouted Wallerstein. "That's your name!"

## World War II and
## Full Frequency Range Recording

After the war, there was another turntable revolution. The disc itself was about to undergo a technological reinvention, sparking an all-out format war between the corporate dynasties CBS and RCA. Until 1948, records played at 78 rpm. Then the LP arrived.

Overall, wartime accelerates the pace of technological development; the turbulent 1940s saw the rise of jet propulsion, atomic power, the first computers, radar, and sound recording on magnetic tape. Tape recorders and superior microphones developed during the war paved the way for high fidelity and stereo. Better-sounding equipment and a new generation of music software—the 33 1/3 rpm long-playing record (LP) and the 45 rpm single—spread a new style of music to a new generation of listeners and consumers, but the transition wasn't easy.

FM radio broadcasts had begun in the late thirties, stimulating the appetite for high-quality sound reproduction among classical music fans. Immediately after World War II, the hi-fi bug bit the British, and wartime technology provided ample means to scratch that itch.

As the war effort accelerated in 1940, English Decca developed full frequency range recording (FFRR). An engineer named Arthur Haddy devised the process, used to train sensor operators to distinguish between British subs and German U-boats. Submarine noises were recorded and stored on discs. These records needed to reproduce a far broader range of sound waves than the standard 78s or transcription discs. Haddy and his squad of British scientists achieved this result through a host of microimprovements, such as cutting smaller grooves into a more durable surface, using a better stylus for playback, and studying and refining the record-duplication process. This multitiered or systems approach relied on teamwork and consistency, as opposed to a lone inventor pursuing the transcendent big breakthrough.

A number of British manufacturers—notably, Garrard—turned to audio products when the demand for war goods dried up. In the United States, a few companies followed suit. Fisher, for example, marketed the first component receivers in 1945. Trading on its wartime research and expertise, English Decca introduced the Piccadilly model phonograph during the 1944 holiday shopping season. For its time, this affordable player delivered great sound and high-tech features: lightweight tonearm, magnetic pickup, and a sapphire stylus. It sounded especially strong with Decca's new high-quality FFRR discs.

The Piccadilly never caught on here, interestingly, because it wasn't sold in the States. But FFRR records did, and as imports they caught on with high-end classical fans known as the carriage trade. Even at a premium price, however, the Piccadilly turntables were never imported.

"Some deal must have been made," speculate British authors Read and Welch in *From Tinfoil to Stereo*.

It was expedient to deny Americans superior equipment at lower prices because they were willing to pay more for less efficient equipment. The introduction of the LP record by Columbia and others in 1948 may well have been a calculated maneuver to dispose of the threat of the European invasion, rather than just a logical step forward in the domestic competition for business.

While the nefarious details of this "deal" will never be known, the precedent set here is obvious. Manipulation of the market-place, by stopping or staggering the commercial acceptance of new technology, became the game plan followed by the entertain-ment industry ever since. The fact that this strategy usually back-fires or often achieves an unintended result makes no difference. Success in this business means figuring out how to harness the force of technological change rather than offering passive resis-tance—and this doesn't occur without a struggle.

The crucial technological development of the World War II era that would shape the phonograph's future was tape recording, and it began in Germany. Overall, Germany outpaced the Allies in sound research and its military application. Two German busi-nesses, the electrical manufacturer AEG and chemical concern I. G. Farben, joined to produce the first high-quality tape recorder, the Magnetophon.

The Nazi regime relied on information technology and propa-ganda; Hitler controlled and seduced the populace with a con-stantly broadcast barrage of hate speech. High-quality tape recorders helped get the message across. Throughout the war, Hitler's omnipresence on German airwaves vexed Allied radio monitors who listened in; at times he seemed to be in two places at once: maybe working with a sound-alike double? Speeches broadcast from two distant cities—Vienna and Munich, say— would occur almost back to back, and both would sound live. The answer came at the end of the war, when U.S. troops raided several German military radio stations and found the secret weapon: several Magnetophon recorders. These machines were brought back and their vacuum tubes and electric motors closely examined. When fed through two tape heads, a simple strip of paper tape coated with a fine layer of brown iron oxide reproduces sound nearly as well as the most advanced disc phonograph system.

By the late 1940s magnetic tape recording caught on with U.S record companies. Tape was quickly adopted as the initial step in the recording process. In the studio, recording on magnetic tape superseded direct recording on blank acetate discs. The advantages were dramatic: tape could run uninterrupted for thirty minutes, it could be played back immediately and, most important, it could be edited. Various segments of tape could be spliced together in perfect continuity, mistakes could be erased and effects (such as echo chamber) could be added. Music on tape could be meticulously worked over before being transferred to disc. At the same time, the flexibility and speed of using magnetic tape made the recording process cheaper and more accessible.

## Enter the LP

The gauntlet was thrown at the Waldorf-Astoria Hotel in New York City. On a summer day in 1948, Columbia Records launched its new record format with a press conference. The long-playing microgroove record, or LP, was pitched as a technological breakthrough, an advance on all fronts. The diameter of this disc—12 inches—was the only nod to convention. Spinning at $33\frac{1}{3}$ rpm, the plastic disc could fit twenty-five minutes of sound per side.

The long player lived up to its name. This was merely five or six times the duration of a standard 78. Columbia's advertisements guaranteed the LP as "nonbreakable." These thin discs were made of black plastic, and vinylite or vinyl replaced the traditional shellac mix. (Union Carbide Corporation introduced vinyl resins in the 1930s.) Since the vinyl disc required a more sensitive stylus with a lighter tracking weight, it wouldn't wear out as fast as the earlier model.

Before Columbia and Goldmark, there had been attempts at extending the length of the record. Edison had offered, in limited quantities, a long-playing version of his Diamond Disc in the 1920s. And RCA Victor briefly floated a 33 $\frac{1}{3}$ rpm disc in 1931. Around the same time, Bell developed an experimental 10-inch LP, intended for use on film soundtracks. Victor too released a limited number of long-playing 78 recordings, mostly classical offerings headed by Leopold Stokowski and the Philadelphia Orchestra. The cardboard package containing these multiple-disc sets became known as an album. The name stuck, but the sound quality stunk. It was a setback, inferior to the appalling cackle of the 78.

But 33 $\frac{1}{3}$ is no magic number. "There is nothing holy about this speed," wrote Goldmark. The old transcription discs for film soundtracks ran at 33 $\frac{1}{3}$ rpm, because that speed enabled the background music in theaters to run as long as the standard movie reel. "I thought the transcription disc was a good starting point from which to build a long-playing record," continued Goldmark, "though I want to clear up an erroneous impression . . . that the speed is the essential fact in long playing. It isn't."

Columbia Records hyped Goldmark's microgroove LP as the new industry standard. For classical music fans, it no doubt represented a great leap forward. An entire symphony could now be contained on one disc, a full movement heard without interruption. The advent of the LP unleashed an avalanche of classical releases.

Shrewdly anticipating the long player, Columbia had been recording duplicate masters of each session on large acetate blanks. By 1948, they had a backlog of noise-free recordings that were readily transferable to the longer format. Columbia issued a list of 101 LP titles at the Waldorf-Astoria event: the initial catalogue included three entire operas (*Hansel and Gretel*, *La Traviata*, *La Boheme*), authoritative recordings of seven out of nine Beethoven symphonies, and so on.

Though classical dominated the early LP market, pop collections from Frank Sinatra, Dinah Shore, Harry James, Xavier Cugat, and others were also dropped into the mix. With an eye toward hardware compatibility, Columbia struck a clever deal with the Philco Company. The new long-playing records could spin on *any* phonograph fitted with a Philco adapter for just $29.95! The "adapter" plugged into existing home phonographs. It consisted of a turntable with cartridge and stylus, all set to accommodate the new format. Enclosed in curved plastic, the units earned the name *clamshell*. No wonder the LP caught on. In the first year of release, sales of "long-playing microgroove recordings" topped $3 million. Columbia's new format was up and running.

## Groove Theory

What was so great about these microgrooves anyway?

First, consider the recording process at that time. It all begins with a microphone. The microphone collects sound vibrations, then converts them into electric currents. Next, the amplifier magnifies those electrical currents and transfers them to the recording head. There the electric currents are converted into mechanical movements: the vibrations of a recording stylus. The wiggling stylus cuts a wavy pattern or groove into a rotating disc. This lacquer or wax plate becomes the template or master disc.

The grooves cut in the master disc accurately follow the shape of the sound waves, visible under a microscope. The high-pitched waves are bunched together and low-pitched waves are spread apart. (As his hearing deteriorated, Edison would issue forth musical evaluations after inspecting his finished cylinder or disc with a microscope.)

Sound is reproduced when a phonograph needle drags through the grooves. Riding across the grooves produces vibrations in the needle, duplicating the pitch and amplitude of the original. The cartridge picks up those vibrations, converting them back into electric signals. The signals are transferred to an amplifier and then liberated via a loudspeaker. *Voilà!*

Before Goldmark, the physical means of recreating sound hadn't been fundamentally altered since the Jazz Age. And the 78 rpm record itself had barely progressed from the format of the 1920s. The opportunity for invention beckoned. Technology was about to catch up with music.

## The Long View

It's a classic American success story: the immigrant made good. Peter Goldmark was born in Budapest, Hungary, in 1906. Educated in Berlin and Vienna, he earned his doctorate in physics from the University of Vienna. (His mother, significantly, was an avid musician.) Entering the United States in 1933, he quickly made his name as an engineer. Initially turned down by RCA, Goldmark was hired by CBS in 1936. Before he masterminded the LP record, Goldmark conducted pioneering work in color television, and several years after, he developed one of the first videocassette systems, Electronic Video Recording (EVR). In the course of his career, Goldmark held over 160 patents.

Yet he never collected royalties on his most profitable invention. The LP patents accrued to the corporation, not the inventor. Speaking in interviews, Dr. Goldmark never comes across as bitter or envious. He always corrects the assumption that he must've struck it rich with the LP, as somebody surely did. He always claimed to relish the complimentary LPs he received in lieu of a royalty check from CBS every month. Perhaps he was being sardonic while at the same time acknowledging the price of corporate support.

Goldmark enjoyed a great run at CBS, thirty-six years. He quickly assumed command of the research labs and embarked on his quest. Until the end of that term, Goldmark was given a wide berth, not to mention financial backing, for his experimentation. He had the luxury to pursue dead ends and learn from mistakes. In 1954, the maverick inventor even installed a custom-designed portable phonograph in the glove compartment of a spanking-new Ford Thunderbird. Yet the microgroove LP stands as Goldmark's masterpiece. He referred to it as a piece of pure technology: invention and development combined.

Peter Goldmark retired from CBS in the late 1960s and set up shop on his own. After years of off-and-on sparring with CEO William Paley, he became bitterly disappointed by the company's lack of support for his EVR videocassette. Clearly, CBS Television felt threatened by the nascent format. Paley ultimately squelched the project. This vote of no confidence convinced the headstrong inventor once and for all that his boss utterly lacked vision. Goldmark maintained the long view on technology to the end of his days.

"The disc and tape will exist side by side," he predicted in 1973.

Neither one of them seems to be replacing the other one. The disc is convenient for choosing a certain selection—which a lot of people prefer. There are ways you could put a whole library on laser disk . . . laser beams. The only problem is, it wouldn't be profitable. People will expect to pay the same for a laser disc that they do for a single piece of music.

Mixing sixties idealism with his pragmatic engineer's outlook, Goldmark presented himself as a futurist in his post-CBS years. His brave new world was both plugged-in and bucolic. He pitched a technological utopian community of his design. This *New Rural Society,* as he billed it, in many respects foretells the ex-urban upper-middle-class neighborhood of the twenty-first century. Strangely enough, Goldmark's dream world closely resembles our nation today: satellite communities united by communications technology. According to Goldmark's plan, most people would live and work in the same place, a not-so-far-out response to sixties urban blight, as it turns out.

"One communications satellite in orbit over the United States could take in all of the important sports, cultural and entertainment events of the cities and make them available to every rural center in the country," declared Goldmark. (At that point, cable TV was only a rumor.) "Ninety-nine percent of people never see a concert, or a live performance of a play or a ballet . . . isn't this much better than not seeing it at all?"

Peter Goldmark died in an automobile accident in December 1977. His passing came exactly 100 years after the invention of the phonograph, the same month that Edison applied for his patents. In terms of music, the magnificence of Goldmark's legacy cannot be overstated. The birth and development of the LP matched the astonishing ascent of the baby boomers step by step. Originally aimed at Broadway and opera lovers, the album format connected with successive generations of young pop listeners. The LP—and the technology that made it possible—stands as the most enduring cultural legacy bequeathed to baby boomers by their parents.

## Battle of the Speeds

William Paley of CBS engaged in an eternal tug-of-war with his crosstown nemesis, David Sarnoff of RCA. In the twenty-first century, what remains of Columbia belongs to Sony (Japan), while Nipper (the dog of Victor fame) now answers to Bertelsmann (Germany). Back in 1948, CBS executives were sweating the competition before they introduced the vaunted LP record. How would their sworn foes at RCA respond? Shrewdly, Paley extended a preemptive invitation to Sarnoff. Why not join forces? Surely, a joint venture between CBS and RCA would enhance—if not ensure—the new format's success.

Once Peter Goldmark had ironed out the technical bugs, the head of RCA was respectfully summoned to CBS headquarters. Sarnoff dutifully attended the LP demonstration along with a team of RCA engineers. Paley and his entourage of suits looked on as Dr. Goldmark conducted a theatrical comparison between a 78 rpm record and the new long-playing format. The scene resembled one of Edison's tone-tests, only this time without the human participant. It was a command performance for the master inventor, and his revolutionary record lived up to its advance billing. The imperious top man at RCA, CBS's biggest competitor, was duly impressed. "Sarnoff was out of his chair," wrote Goldmark. "The effect was electrifying."

When Sarnoff called back in a few days, however, the unthinkable happened again. He turned the deal down flat.

Why? Perhaps that failed attempt in 1931 explains it. In retrospect, RCA Victor's response to the LP qualifies as perverse. Rather than jump on the bandwagon, in January 1949, RCA brought out its own innovation: the 45 rpm microgroove record.

The RCA engineers assigned a code name to the 45 rpm project: Madame X. The sound quality was equal to the LP. Unfortunately, the duration of the 45 rpm disc ran just as long as a conventional 78, four minutes, tops. Measuring only 7 inches in diameter, 45 rpm discs used a large center hole, so playing 45s on a regular turntable required a larger spindle. This was intended to accelerate the record-changing time—"instantaneous," according to the hype. Yet by Goldmark's stopwatch measure, exacting to be sure, the music-to-music pause on RCA's new mini-discs lasted for eight agonizing seconds. Classical music was *doomed* on 45s.

Despite this failing, RCA soldiered on. In the 45 rpm format, longer works (such as symphonies) came packaged in multidisc albums that supposedly "fit on your shelf." These 45 rpm records played on a special unit, much like the Philco clamshell. Offered at $12.95, these plug-in turntables came fitted with "the world's fastest record changer." A larger center space, of course, made 45s impossible to play on the same turntable as a 33 $\frac{1}{3}$ record, and this may well be the real story behind the donut hole.

Yet even faster record changing was probably cold comfort to a music-crazed public suddenly faced with a confusing, contradictory array of choices. This format war was a maddening free-for-all. Lasting only a year, it caused not only havoc with consumers but considerable damage to the industry. In the short run, everybody lost something in the battle of the speeds. In 1947, the value of the retail record business was estimated at $204 million. By 1949, that figure had slipped to $157,875,000. Confusion over competing formats had to have had something to do with it. Anarchy reigned over the recording industry, at least for awhile.

"One speed is all you need!" Columbia's hype proclaimed, further fanning the flames. During one CBS-sponsored promotion, Sam Goody stores in New York City "gave away" the adapters—with a $25 purchase of LPs. Even today, it doesn't sound like such a bad deal.

RCA spent $5 million on their ad campaign. But by 1950, they were already making 33 $\frac{1}{3}$ rpm LPs as well as 45s. According to legend, Arturo Toscanini pressured Sarnoff and RCA to adapt the LP format. Apparently, the great conductor didn't appreciate the interruptions any more than Peter Goldmark did.

One year after RCA caved on the LP, Columbia began producing 45s.

Decca and Mercury gravitated toward the LP format. Capitol hedged its bets by making records in all three formats: In 1950, the Los Angeles–based upstart sent forth a Hollywood String Quartet release on 33⅓, 45, and 78.

At the same time, London's EMI Records were repulsed by the battle across the sea. The British firm vowed to stick with the 78 format, at least until affairs proceeded in more seemly fashion. In the event that it did switch formats, EMI promised to alert the British buying public and even give six months' notice. Two years later, this is precisely what happened. Predictably, the rest of Europe fell like dominoes: France, Spain, Germany. Long-playing records became the dominant format. Even the USSR State Music Trust issued an LP catalogue, in 1953. Though other record companies adopted the LP format, one by one they picked up the 45 format too and applied it to nonclassical releases—that is, popular music.

Rebuilt at two speeds, the phonograph industry thus turned into a pop music machine during the second half of the 1950s. Writing in *The American Popular Music Business in the 20th Century*, Russell Sanjek summarizes the situation with biblical wisdom. "The manufacturers of phonographs . . . made a Solomon-like decision, and used both [speeds]."

As the battle of the speeds wound down, Goldmark and his associates developed a turnaround stylus with dual speed. This gave CBS the advantage of marketing a universal instrument: a turntable that played at either speed. Hardware compatability allows for coexistence between rival software formats, once the format wars are over.

And coexistence was indeed possible. By 1953, RCA had sold ten million 45 rpm phonographs. The shorter duration and higher quality of the 45 rpm record was perfectly suited to pop songs. That market had grown somewhat stagnant in the late forties; as the swing generation grew up, musical tastes changed, and the cost of maintaining a big band grew prohibitive. This downturn wouldn't last long. The payoff would come a few years later with the rise of rock 'n' roll and RCA's recording superstar, Elvis Presley.

The 45 rpm format turned out to be a wise short-term investment. Phonograph sales grew exponentially from 1952 to 1954, though they still lagged below the highs of 1947. Perhaps the battle of the speeds represents a healthy bout of competition, the technological version of an adolescent rite of passage. It was surely a bumpy transition.

## Hi-Fi at Home

The first LP to reach one million sales was the original-cast recording of *Oklahoma!* Decca released its hit version of this Rodgers and Hammerstein musical in 1949. Sales had reached fifteen million by 1958. The advent of the LP format touched off a craze for albums of Broadway and movie music. *Kiss Me Kate* and *South Pacific* followed *Oklahoma.* The *South Pacific* movie soundtrack from 1958 became the highest-selling LP of the decade.

Broadway soundtracks offered continuity in addition to a catered menu of catchy songcraft. That consistent quality lifted those fifties original-cast LPs above their pop competition. Most early long players barely deserve the term *album*; these LPs are motley grab bags featuring a couple of hits tucked away in moth-balls. When Frank Sinatra switched from Columbia to Capitol in the mid 1950s, all that changed in a hurry. Working with such arrangers as Nelson Riddle and Billy May, Sinatra issued a golden thread of thematic LPs: *In the Wee Small Hours, Songs for Swingin' Lovers*, and the masterpiece *Frank Sinatra Sings for Only the Lonely.*

Freedom from the 78 format meant more room for improvisation. Jazz musicians thrived on LPs. Comedy records—later called stand-up, or spoken-word albums—enjoyed a commercial vogue at the end of the 1950s. The wry and buttoned-down Bob Newhart watched no doubt bemused as his album releases climbed to the top of the pop charts in 1960. Even the scathing Lenny Bruce was able to record a (nonobscene) series of LPs.

The acceptance of the LP format also spurred the rapid growth of the hi-fi component industry. As more sound was crammed into a record's grooves, more electronic equipment was required to coax it out. Audiophiles began to multiply. Special records had to be manufactured to fulfill their peculiar needs. Mercury announced its line of Living Presence LPs. London (American Decca) rightfully boasted of its FFRR (Full Frequency Range Recording) LPs. Columbia featured its own futuristic-sounding 360 Sound, while RCA dipped into the history books for New Orthophonic High Fidelity. An LP bearing one of these imprints is likely to contain a bombastic performance of "Also Sprach Zarathustra" or the "1812 Overture."

In the long run, everybody gained something from the battle of the speeds as well. The rapidly growing number of phonographs in American homes created a solid technological base for another musical revolution. Before ambitious long-playing records and elaborate stereo phonographs ushered in the golden age of the rock album, however, something more elemental had to occur. A confluence of catchy 45 rpm singles and cheap transistor radios gave birth to rock 'n' roll.

## chapter 4

# PONYTAIL RIBBONS, POPSICLES, AND PEANUT BRITTLE

> High school is where the middle-aged businessman happened. He was a manager, agent, producer, disc jockey or general hustler.
>
> —Nik Cohn, *Rock from the Beginning*

THIS IS A TALE OF TWO DJS. One couldn't have existed without the other. Between them, they remade popular music and the business surrounding it. One claimed to have invented rock 'n' roll, the other discovered a gold mine. Spinning records on the turntable led to bigger and (sometimes) better things for both. Alan Freed pursued the standard spin-offs: promoting concerts and portraying himself in movies. Ultimately felled by scandal, he became a legend, a symbol of rock 'n' roll's rebel spirit, the man who spread the word. What Dick Clark did with rock 'n' roll and television on *American Bandstand* was to forge a natural connection by finding the right audience. It was absurd, simple beauty: Clark played records while teenage couples danced. On that foundation, he proceeded to construct an empire.

Both men were called before Congress to testify on corruption—payola—in the record and radio business. In the end, one man was ruined while the other emerged unscathed. The so-called payola scandal was a sidetrack for Dick Clark, a temporary setback.

*Payola* equals *pay* plus *Victrola*. Actually, the practice—guaranteeing airplay for records with bribes and coveted favors—had been around nearly as long as the Nipper logo. In the Tin Pan Alley era, freelance salesmen known as *song pluggers* worked the music publishers just like independent promoters service radio stations today. Inevitably, in the bad old days, cash would change hands. By the 1950s, the practice got out of hand. Indeed, what happened was that the practice got *organized*: A few extra records and maybe a hi-fi set on holidays for a DJ turned into regular cash outlays. The pay-for-play racket ran regularly, like a clock—or rather, like payoffs to the mob for protection. This under-the-table bonanza erupted just as rock 'n' roll hit its freewheeling stride in the fifties. The double whammy of the devil's music and dubious business practices triggered a congressional investigation.

Today, Dick Clark is still around. So are his musical progeny, the teen idols, still singing their disposable tunes and releasing hour-long CDs of hit plus filler. Only music television, that glowing cross-media contradiction, has changed beyond recognition since the days of *American Bandstand*. Or has it?

The A side of this story has to be Dick Clark. His role is the prospector, pitchman, master of ceremonies, survivor. His broadcast manner is calm and reassuring. He recognized rock 'n' roll as a deep and previously untapped source of enrichment. Dick Clark discovered the booming buying power of teenagers, and built a multimedia marketplace that still thrives today. The B side is Alan Freed. His role is the unruly creative force, the musical innovator and tragic hero. On the air, he's in your face, brash and stimulating. He mesmerized a young, white audience merely by spinning records—those by black R&B groups. Alan Freed may not have "invented" rock 'n' roll, but he nurtured and furthered it.

As myth has it, Freed visited Leo Mintz's record shop in Cleveland one day in 1951, while working at WJW. There Freed saw white teenagers browsing the R&B racks and dancing. Clearly, he fell in love with the new sounds: Red Prysock, Big Al Sears, and Ivory Joe Hunter were his favorites. But those bin flippers were most likely black, according to Freed's biographer, John A. Jackson. The white audience, and notoriety, came later.

To many ears, pioneering DJ Alan Freed went so far as to emulate and flat-out imitate the fast-rapping style of the black R&B DJs. The barking Moondog wasn't alone. There were black-sounding white DJs on many R&B stations during the fifties, including "Daddy" Gene Nobles and "John R" Richbourg in Memphis, Hunter Hancock in Los Angeles, "Poppa Stoppa" (Clarence Hayman) in New Orleans, and more. And they were popular with blacks and a growing number of young whites.

During the rise of rock 'n' roll, even before Dick Clark, *American Bandstand* capitalized on teenage dance crazes, from the innocuous bunny hop to the mild hip-shaking R&B-derived steps such as bop and stroll. With laserlike precision, each *Bandstand*-endorsed dance trend was tied to a custom-built song on 45, often released by Philly-based labels such as Cameo-Parkway.

Overall, record sales quadrupled in the years following the war, jumping from roughly $100 million in 1945 to $500 million in 1958. After World War II, there was an explosion of R&B

records on independent labels, so Alan Freed had much to be enthused about—and a great deal of records from which to choose. The best sounding of these came from regional establishments such as Atlantic in New York (R&B), Chess in Chicago (blues and R&B), King in Cincinnati (both R&B and country), and thousands of local one-shots. Thanks to the technological advances of the 1940s and the advent of tape recording, the studio became accessible to all in the fifties. Producing a cheap record was easy; getting it heard, however, was more complicated—but not impossible.

Alan Freed hotly denied the payola charges in 1959. "If I've helped somebody, I'll accept a nice gift, but I won't take a dime to plug a record. I'd be a fool to; I'd be giving up control of my program." That same year, Dick Clark offered a different line of defense. He didn't need the money; the sly *Bandstand* host was working every available angle. "I proceeded to get into talent management, music publishing, record pressing, label making, distribution, domestic and foreign rights, motion pictures, show promotions and teenage merchandising."

One established way of paying gratitude was to give DJs some of the publishing rights to a song. It was a wheel of fortune that successful DJs—including Alan Freed—kept right on spinning until the payola scandal forced them to stop (or at least be discreet). In 1955, Freed "cowrote," or got a cut of, the rock 'n' roll classic "Maybellene" by Chess artist Chuck Berry. Ironically, it was a big hit in its original (black) version, eclipsing any cover attempt. According to Freddie "Boom Boom" Cannon, *Bandstand*'s Clark earned his cowriting credits with canny commercial input. The guy knew how to not only bait a hook but also reel it in.

The scandal represented the last stand of Tin Pan Alley against the rising tide of a new popular music. It was essentially a grudge match: The American Society of Composers, Authors and Publishers against Broadcast Music International. ASCAP was a traditional publishing organization of old-time songwriters; BMI was a postwar upstart publisher of rock 'n' roll, R&B, and country artists. (A DJ such as Freed would have relied on BMI-licensed records almost exclusively.) ASCAP accused BMI of using payola to achieve market dominance—and even worse, foisting inferior, offensive music onto innocent ears.

In March 1958, a station owner named Todd Storz held a weekend convention at a hotel in Kansas City, Missouri, for radio and record people. Mitch Miller, then head of artists and repertoire for Columbia Records, gave a hectoring speech. The respected record man lectured the radio men, claiming they'd "abdicated" their birthright. According to Miller, the choice of records they played were strictly for the rabble—"the eight to fourteen year olds, the pre-shave crowd that makes up 12% of the population and zero percent of its buying power, once you eliminate the ponytail ribbons, Popsicles and peanut brittle." Over time, the music business would stop singing along with Mitch and start milking that audience for all it was worth.

In the wake of the TV quiz show scandal and investigation, Congress decided to dig in. A probe was announced on November 16, 1959. House Subcommittee Legislative Oversight Hearings began in February 1958. Dozens of DJs testified; both Clark and Freed appeared and faced the music.

Before the actual House hearings began, the payola investigations had already kicked up a lot of dirt. Alan Freed got fired from WABC when he refused to sign a generic in-house disclaimer about taking payola. All the on-air employees that could possibly be tainted had to sign—save one. Dick Clark cut his own deal.

Ultimately, Clark was required to divest many of his holdings. As to whether he showed favoritism toward certain recordings while programming *Bandstand*, none could be certain. During the hearings, Clark acknowledged that he had partial copyright to 150 or more songs, including many that had been played on *Bandstand*. Was it a conflict of interest, or more like a convergence of interest?

Payola in its classic, crudest form—"bribes, booze and broads" in addition to drugs—went underground. It even flourished again for a time in the go-go, greed-is-good 1980s. But the lasting effect of the payola scandal has been an insidious diminishing of the DJs musical role on the radio.

## The 45 rpm Revolution

Victory in a format war doesn't eliminate the losing technology completely; instead, the other way of doing things often settles into a niche, where it can generate profits for a long time to come.

Gradually, the deadly competition mutated into a complex and complimentary relationship. Radio and record players became interdependent, and the rise of rock 'n' roll depended on both mediums. Just as radio depended on records to fill airtime, the record industry came to depend on radio for exposure and promotion.

The flip side of high fidelity was a 45 rpm revolution. Though the 33⅓ LP won the battle of the speeds, the losing 7-inch format found its killer application in the aftermath. The teenage rock 'n' roll explosion was born of R&B and country & western delivered on 7-inch 45 rpm records, nurtured by radio disc jockeys, and propelled by transistor radios and portable record players. The rise of rock 'n' roll neatly coincided with a demographic growth spurt now known as the baby boom; this mixed message of radio and records and ubiquity of styles—a constant drumbeat—subtly worked against the prevailing atmosphere of racial segregation, subverting it from within.

The requirements of radio shaped the form of the rock 'n' roll single, and as radio lost its mass audience to television during the 1950s, the booming sound of rock 'n' roll offered radio access to a new demographic. Not just the new (white) youth market, but ethnic listeners too.

By 1954, 700 radio stations were addressing the black audience. Anyone could tune in, of course, and in a few years, it seemed like everyone did—everyone under thirty, anyway. Independent stations were gradually replacing the big radio networks; they efficiently serviced the R&B and country markets, spinning records from a growing number of independent record companies. Famously, Atlantic Records made its name with genre-defining R&B and soul out of New York City, nominally still with us today in conglomerated form. Regional record companies specialized in local delicacies from New Orleans (Minit), Houston (Duke), and Los Angeles (Modern, Alladin). Chess pumped Chicago blues, and Cincinnati's King covered the bases with Cowboy Copas and Hank Ballard. Regional specialties reached broad audiences through radio. So-called minority tastes became majority fare.

The major labels—RCA, Columbia, Decca, and Capitol—didn't turn a deaf ear to this trend. They responded with cover versions; the act of white musicians rerecording successful songs by blacks had been a tradition since the 1890s. Releasing mainstream versions of specialty-market hits was a cheap and efficient ploy for the big companies. This practice wasn't strictly racial, either; as country (formerly hillbilly) music boomed alongside R&B, the likes of Patti Page and Frankie Laine delivered detwanged covers of the originals. The proliferation of cheaper recording technology led to a flood of copycat records. The act of mechanical reproduction reinforced the art (and commerce) of the cover versions.

One classic example is "Open the Door, Richard," a vaudeville number identified with the performer "Dusty" Fletcher. Variations on this coming-home-drunk routine had been in circulation since at least the early 1930s. Dusty released his version of "Richard" on National in 1947. He wasn't alone. One dozen competing cover versions appeared during that year. Eventually, Count Basie (on Columbia) and Louis Jordan (on Decca) both rode the song onto the pop charts—another key crossover along the lines of Mamie Smith's "Crazy Blues" back in the twenties. Bob Dylan and the Band even alluded to "Richard" on *The Basement Tapes*. The late forties cover version phenomenon reinforces the mechanical, repetitive nature of recording. Quantity begins to overrule quality. Popular singers now became interchangeable; surely songs must be next.

By 1950, recorded music was a staple of radio broadcasts, but it wasn't yet a purely automated process. A human being was required to play the records—and as soon as people began to publicly manipulate the turntable, the far-flung jumble of American popular music began its spectacular mutation into rock 'n' roll.

## The Pancake Flippers

At first, the turntable hands belonged to bland announcers or blatant hacks: musicians union flunkies inserted in pseudo-jobs derisively referred to as pancake flippers. Gradually these short-order servers expanded their role and repertoire by not just changing records but choosing them. The pancake flipper became the disc jockey, a succulent handle spun by a *Variety* reporter in 1941 (*record jockey* had appeared in 1940). Soon thereafter, an anonymous shadow morphed into a man of power and influence in the music industry.

Disc jockeys could even rise above their stations. On the way up, the DJ functioned as tastemaker, trendsetter, gatekeeper, and money grabber. The very best DJs elevated the act of selecting and presenting records and turned pancake flipping into an art form. When the radio DJ's job regressed to a semiautomated form of announcing, by the late 1960s, a new breed of creative turntable jockeys emerged in the discotheques and on the streets.

Radio was the genesis of mass communications; it also gave birth to mass marketing. The commercial heyday of rock 'n' roll DJs heralds the enduring reign of the Top 40—and the development of a vast, previously untapped commercial resource, the *teenage* pop music market. Portable record players, 45 rpm singles, and transistor radios provide the driving technological forces behind this commercial revolution. But the disc jockey's story stretches back well before the late 1950s.

Martin Block must be declared the first true recognizable radio DJ, as we know it today. He negotiated a tricky double role, that of self-styled musical maven and master salesman. From February

3, 1935, to 1950, his program *The Make-Believe Ballroom* enchanted listeners to New York's WNEW.

Simultaneously, *The Lucky Strike Hit Parade* (also known as *Your Hit Parade*) aired every Saturday on the nationwide NBC Red Network. Between the two, a new standard of pop music success was set. It was an efficient little system, a way for radio to program records and measure popular tastes at the same time. The hit parade format may not exactly have been scientific, but it certainly opened the new medium for selling pop music.

Block prided himself not just on musical knowledge but also on the power of his pitch. He took credit for coining a couple of the classic telegraphic tobacco pitches—LSMFT (Lucky Strike Means Fine Tobacco) and ABC (Always Buy Chesterfields). One year he even sold refrigerators, as self-generated legend has it, during an upstate snowstorm. On the air, Block really would make-believe. Rather than tally a Top 10, he pretended to be a bandleader, addressing the listeners personally in his own crooner's timbre.

Martin Block also pioneered the still-lucrative practice of radio syndication. In 1948, he earned nearly $2 million for selling *Make-Believe Ballroom* to thirty stations around the country. Six years later, he signed a million-dollar contract with ABC. Even though Block missed the boat on rock 'n' roll, his national success with such a simple format set a precedent, one that still shapes what we hear on the air today. Music sells the product, and the DJ sells the sounds.

James Caesar Petrillo fought in vain. Canned music dominated radio programming in the early fifties. Todd Storz distilled the loose hit parade formula into a taut, foolproof format: the Top

40. Before that, radio offered a hodgepodge of musical styles and programming. Storz owned a number of stations around the country, including the first station to exclusively devote itself to pop music, Omaha's KOWH in Nebraska, beginning in 1949. With all the copycat and cover records floating around, the Top 40 programs performed a vital function: choosing the "best" version and ignoring the others. The Top 40 stations didn't only play the hits, they fostered an illusion of selectivity, in essence recreating the jukebox effect. Storz built the framework in the early 1950s during the dull reign of smooth pop singers such as Frankie Laine and Kitty Kallen. The structure was in place.

When rock came along, the Top 40 rolled over. In 1955, the Storz-owned WHB in Kansas City became the first station to play all rock 'n' roll, and rock-dominated Top 40 programming spread across the country.

More accessible than a jukebox, Top 40 radio subverted the very notions of choice and musical taste. Top 40 radio stations substituted the DJ's (in reality, the programmer's) assumption in place of consumers' selection. The pancake flippers took over for the coin droppers.

After the dust of the payola scandal settled, radio DJs returned to merely flipping pancakes and running their mouths. Even as they lost the power to pick and choose records, the DJs began to wield a different brand of power: utter verbal anarchy. Taking a page from the mad-rapping R&B jockeys of the fifties, your average Top 40 DJ of the mid sixties was a helium-voiced microphone fiend. He sputtered away in rapid-fire volleys that crackled audibly across the tinny, echo-laden frequencies of a transistor radio. Breathless, hypnotizing, hysteria inducing, his between-song patter must be considered an early form of rap. Unlike the syncopated flow of a late sixties jock, it seemed to exist in a separate sphere from the music it accompanied.

The jocks used songs as a springboard into the ozone. Every market had its exemplars, but the king of kamikaze Top 40 had to be New York City's Murray Kaufmanns, a.k.a. Murray the K. Like all disc jockeys, Murray hopped from station to station. His peak was on WINS in the mid 1960s, when he famously ingratiated himself with the Beatles at their first U.S. press conference and proceeded to ride their coattails to something resembling fame and fortune. Dubbing himself "the Fifth Beatle," Murray focused his radio show and amphetamine verbal shtick almost exclusively on the Fab Four. Somewhat aghast, New Journalist Tom Wolfe fired off a famous 1965 profile of Murray the K.

> The radio is now something people listen to while they're doing something else . . . [the kids] are outside, all over the place, tooling around in automobiles, lollygagging around with transistors plugged into their skulls, listening to the radio. Listening is not exactly the word. They use the radio as a background, as an aural prop for whatever kind of life they want to imagine they're leading. They don't want any messages at all, they want an atmosphere. Half the time, as soon as they get a message—namely a commercial or a news spot—they start turning the dial, looking for the atmosphere they lost. So there are all these kids out there somewhere, roaming all over the dial, looking for something that will hook not the minds but the psyche.

Typically bizarre sixties footnote: When people finally tired of the Beatle gimmick, Murray the K dropped it. Then he reappeared in love beads. Unbelievably, he helped to invent the rambling "progressive rock" format at New York's WOR just months later.

Overall, the heyday of hysterical DJs didn't last long. By 1966, AM radio was turning into a lean, quiet purring machine thanks to a man named Bill Drake. He began at KYA San Francisco and started a syndicate, Boss Radio. In Drake's hands, the Top 40 format became an airtight system, elevating radio programming into a social science. For all practical purposes, Drake eliminated DJs—or at least recast them as robots.

A former DJ himself, beginning in Donaldsville, Georgia, Drake was the first successful Top 40–programming consultant. He remade rock 'n' roll radio in a fast-paced, clean-cut mode, eliminating its shrieking excesses—along with its personality. Drake instituted many of the practices still in use today: a tighter playlist, tightly reined-in disc jockeys, and continuous market research conducted through listener surveys and focus groups. "Much more music" (and less chatter) was a Drake tag line, yet he cut back on the number of records a station could play. The Top 40 became the Boss 30, supplemented by a handful of "hit bound" new releases and occasional oldies.

"We work a little in reverse," Drake told reporter Harry Shearer in 1967,

> trying to find out what the public wants, and then trying to create that. For instance, by finding out why people tune out a station. It's actually even a subliminal area that we try to go into,

and precise attention is paid to the placement of everything. There's a *great* amount of emphasis on keeping it CLEAN.

All the surveys and research created a vicious circle: If the results show that people don't like unfamiliar records, then stations would play fewer records and play them as often as possible. The systematic and relentless repetition of the Top 40 operates on the assumption that people tune in for short stretches, while riding in the car, for example. On the air, the DJs would function as announcer clones, stripped of even the pretense of tastemaking power. By design, all those zippy station jingles, solid gold weekends, million-dollar contests, and "insane" promotions started to sound the same.

While this spelled short-term success for many of Drake's clients, he ignored the shifting currents in rock 'n' roll. Drake concentrated on hit singles, using sales figures as his main criteria, just as album sales began to overtake singles in the later 1960s. Aesthetically, the move toward complexity and ambition in rock was about to render the Top 40 irrelevant; AM radio retreated to the land of lowest common denominator, the province of preteens and old fogies.

The Beatles became a new kind of celebrity, reinventing the pop music scene in the process. Rather than be co-opted by Hollywood like Elvis Presley, they nudged rock 'n' roll into its next phase: serious, self-conscious, conceptual, and grand. Their audience and their peers gladly followed. FM radio—with its full stereo sound and large number of underutilized stations—was the natural outlet for this latest revolution. Murray the K, the Fifth Beatle himself, was ahead of this curve. Moving to New York's

WOR in late 1966, he led the station into uncharted waters: a roster of hip, knowledgeable DJs playing not just singles but an eclectic mix of album tracks. Barely a year later, the station's owners hired Bill Drake and Murray's grand experiment was over. But the die was cast.

Out on the West Coast, San Francisco's booming underground heralded a new age in rock—and a disaffected DJ gave it a new outlet. A dropout from the Top 40 station KYA, Tom Donahue was hatching his own format in 1967: free-form, antiformula radio for freaks and heads and anybody else burned out by stations where "the hits . . . just keep on coming." First on KMPX and later on KSAN, Donahue and his fellow DJs established an anything-goes style that reflected the loosened strictures of the hippie era. Instead of sounding like they'd been inhaling helium, these jocks seemed to be exhaling pot smoke as they explored the furthest reaches of their musical taste. This was the polar opposite of Bill Drake and his tune-out phobia.

"Most people are button pushers," Donahue said in 1967. "Man, I hear my old lady or my kids create a whole show of their own. When a record ends, they start pushing buttons till they find something else they like." Instead of regurgitating the listeners' preferences, the free-form DJs attempted to transport listeners to a higher plane. For all that lofty ambition, however, Donahue also offered a technological assessment of the new rock's spreading popularity. "I knew that FM stereo would be dominant in five years," he declared in that same interview, "because of everybody's interest in improving sound. Rock record producers are the first people to realize the possibilities of stereo."

The heyday of true free-form FM was even shorter than that of the hysterical Top 40 jocks. As albums came to dominate the marketplace and hippie music conquered the mainstream, the freak-friendly FM stations adopted playlists, program directors, and promotional campaigns of their own. The emergence of FM radio and progressive rock neatly coincided with the widespread accessibility of stereo record players and affordable hi-fi components. By the late sixties, every dorm room had a decent sound system. As the baby-boom generation grew up, their audio hardware choices followed suit: the compact stereo set with FM radio and detachable speakers replaced the quaint "kiddy player" and transistor radio of days gone by. Only one problem lingered. Great stereo sound was now accessible, but it wasn't really portable.

## Transistors

The Top 40 revolution was sparked by transistors, yet another postwar technological innovation. Developed at Bell Labs in the late forties, the transistor circuit eventually brought high fidelity into millions of homes. Transistors (miniscule wire threads) replaced vacuum tubes; they were more reliable, less expensive, smaller, and easier to mass-produce. Even more important, transistors rendered phonographs portable and radios mobile. They also required less power; transistor radios could run on car batteries. Crucially, transistor circuits didn't generate light and heat or burn out the way vacuum tubes did.

Japanese engineers and entrepreneurs first recognized the vast mass-market possibilities in these miniscule electronic devices.

Miniaturization means mega-appeal: accessibility, affordability, efficiency, simplicity, and yes, disposability. In 1957, the Sony Company of Japan offered a transistor radio small enough to fit in a pocket. Six million transistor radios were imported to the United States in 1959, with more than twelve million in use by year's end. Mobile listening fit right into the adolescent lifestyle and, many would say, enhanced it.

Yet radio only stoked the desire for music. It took a while, but the phonograph—now the record player—was remade to accommodate the teenage lifestyle. The battle of the speeds had barely ended when Columbia Records introduced a portable record player in 1953. A boxlike compact, the Columbia 360 was intended as a table model; it wasn't a portable per se because the lid had no latch. *High Fidelity* magazine described it upon release as an "inexpensive portable phonograph with some pretension to high fidelity, good enough to serve as a 'second phonograph' for audiophiles who wanted to take their music on vacation with them or to equip their rumpus room for their youngsters." According to Columbia's own press release, the end result was "high-fidelity in a hatbox." Presciently, the 360 featured two speakers (years before stereo) and played records at all speeds.

The coming generation didn't inherit many pretensions to high fidelity. Sound quality was a functional consideration, not an aesthetic one. Cheap, efficient portable players communicated the rhythmic thump of rock 'n' roll records as well as the console in the living room, if not better. By 1957, RCA Victor offered a portable record player for $39.95; ironically, perhaps, this one-speed 45 rpm machine was dubbed the Victrola. "Now more than ever 45 is your best buy," crowed the accompanying ad copy. But the audience for this revolutionary machine couldn't be audiophiles; they'd already rejected 7-inch extended-play (EP) classical music, after all. The advent of rock 'n' roll created a seemingly permanent niche for the 45 rpm format.

The commercial success of transistor radio led to the application of the microtechnology to record players during the early 1960s. Transistors reduced both the size and cost of audio components, making stereo sound accessible to all. Reduced size made stacking possible. Rather than dominating a room, a stereo system could now be contained on a bookshelf or in a corner. Stereos soon would be even cheap enough for kids. Gathering around the hulking wooden console in the family room was replaced by having your own lightweight plastic model in the bedroom.

Radio assumed a supplemental role during the FM rock era, seldom selected on the stereo, but a mainstay in the car. Mobility and a semicaptive audience kept radio alive. As digital technology rewired the music industry (again), radio faced its own transformation. The demand is still out there. In 1999, the average American listened to more than two hours of radio per day. In 2001, more than 10,000 licensed radio stations shared the airwaves in the United States alone.

## Station to Station

Radio on the Internet sounded like a contradiction at first. Broadcasting is all about mass appeal, seeking the lowest common denominator. The web, though, has come to define narrowcasting— that is, creating custom content for specialized interests. Net radio is in place but not yet popular or profitable. In 2001, radio on the web accounted for only 4 percent of the U.S. market. Tellingly, at the same time, one-third of all conventional stations were also transmitting or streaming over the Internet. Naturally, the World Wide Web offers maximum selection: myriad channels streaming from exotic locales. So far, its allure may be limited to the overzealous and underoccupied. But Net radio boasts the proven draw of secondary use. You can listen while working on your personal computer.

Then the clampdown was enforced. A familiar foe threatened the future existence of Internet radio in 2002. Under a 1998 law, record companies and recording artists were entitled to royalties on every song played on Net radio, or *web cast*. The U.S. copyright office haggled over fees for months, while pro–Internet radio protests were mounted. Record companies and certain artists (such as Don Henley) lobbied for higher fees, of course, but the eventual outcome seemed inevitable. Just paying the originally proposed fee of 14¢ per song would effectively bankrupt most Internet radio outlets because the web casters were strictly small-time independent operators who created a niche and then filled it. Adding insult to injury, the new law allowed traditional broadcast stations to continue doing what they've always done, paying royalties to composers only, not to musicians or record companies. Soon, Internet stations will pay for something the broadcast stations get for free.

The broadcasting landscape has been forcibly remade by another recent legal decision. The Telecommunications Act of 1996 upended the rules about single ownership of multiple stations. The limit of forty stations was dropped, and the entire market quickly clotted into chains held by four conglomerates. Incredibly, one company has come to dominate the entire field. Clear Channel Communications of San Antonio, Texas, owns about 1,200 stations around the country.

The overall effect on programming has been predictable, with central control tightening the existing formats to the breaking point. Consolidation means a handful of programmers decide what more than a thousand stations will play. A practice called *voice tracking* transmits big-city DJ voices to smaller markets; with local references, news, and weather smoothly inserted at the breaks, listeners are none the wiser. Uniformity of programming gained further reinforcement from technological developments. Like every other business in the late 1990s, radio stations converted to digital.

Conventional radio stations increasingly rely on computers. Their music is stored digitally on a hard drive while computer software enacts the once-sacred ritual of song selection. The DJ's job has progressed from pancake flipper to baby-sitter. Rather than seduce the listeners, DJs now serve as caretakers for their computers. They exist to service the very machines that once served them.

A day's worth of music and related content (that is, advertising) can be programmed in just three hours. The entire process is automated: the computer spins the hits and picks the platters. The station's hard drive contains not only a choice of songs but commercials and promotions too. Hard copy printouts help the DJ monitor the program. An override function of course is provided, in case of system failure. The DJ can take over manually and revert to CDs if the computer fails.

DJs can also operate the system semiautomatically, jumping in from time to time to deliver the news or heaven forbid, actually identify a song. Though a DJ is nominally in charge of the music, the computer never rests.

## Satellites

Even at this nascent stage, the technological competition never sleeps either. Satellite radio looms as a challenge to Internet radio. Since mobility ensures radio's survival, the promise of satellite radio is *enhanced* mobility. Not-so-bold prediction: Net radio won't catch on until cars are truly Internet-accessible or a mobile listening device is developed. Accessing the Internet still isn't as easy as switching on a standard old-fashioned radio.

Satellite radio is another story. Actual satellites beam digital-quality audio into your car, for a price. Multiple signals, it is promised, will foil the interference of tunnels and mountains. No doubt modeled on cable television, satellite radio offers a dizzying array of microprogrammed channels for a reasonable monthly subscription fee (around $10). Digital broadcast technology also enhances existing outlets, making AM sound like FM and FM sound like a CD. Or so it is claimed.

As a business, satellite radio was closely attended at its birth. Two companies—Sirius and XM—won a highly restricted federal license. This tightly monitored market was tagged a *duopoly* in the press. Sirius and XM both launched in early. The two services are virtually identical, offering a wide range—100 channels—of narrow-cast stations for $10 to $13 a month. A constant flow of distant and exotic sounds gets cut with talk, the traditional radio filler. Oddly absent on satellite radio is local news, weather, traffic information, and some popular public radio programs. This omission may prove ominous, because the automobile is the raison d'être of satellite radio.

Stationary use is an afterthought, though at least one company planned to market a home computer receiver that looked like a regular radio with dials. With 200 million cars on the road at any given time in America and four million new ones added each year, it's a sizable market. Wisely, the fledgling satellite providers formed alliances with the automobile giants: Sirius with Ford and Chrysler, XM with Honda and General Motors. Supposedly, a "bi" unit—one that receives both services—will be manufactured in 2003. Of course, compatibility is crucial. In 2002, satellite radio was included only as a top-end option on new Cadillacs. Meanwhile, major electronics manufacturers are pushing new satellite units and add-on modules for older cars. By 2003, XM enjoyed a commanding lead over Sirius in the satellite radio stakes. XM boasted half a million subscribers, while Sirius could claim only 30,000. Aiming for a mass market, XM placed its radios in Avis rental cars and Wal Mart stores. Even though XM thrived in comparison with its twin competitor, neither service was expected to turn a profit anytime soon.

One significant doubt remains. Will people pay for something they've been getting for free? Satellite radio offers a great selection of stations, but the selection of music is still made by somebody else. The players in the satellite radio business are banking millions on yes to that question. Stay tuned, because this same question resurfaces during the ultimate format war.

Digital radio in one format or another—via telephone lines or communication satellites—will find its niche in a new century. In the end, radio might even outlive the phonograph—albeit in a form that its inventors couldn't have intended or imagined.

chapter 5

# DREAMING IN STEREO

> I looked at the crank phonograph and I said, "Jesus, if
> Edison can record on that thing, I must be able to, too."
>
> —Les Paul

IN THE 1920S, deep in the Midwest, a teenager tinkered with
every machine in the house. Born in 1915, the precocious Lester
Polsfuss (later Polfuss) already exhibited the intuitive skills of musician and engineer.

At first, his experiments were crude but apparently effective.
Young Lester amplified his guitar through the family Victrola, in-
serting the phonograph needle into the top of a guitar's body.
Turn that on instead of a record, and you get a hell of a noise. So
our junior inventor filled his guitar with rags and sealed it with
plaster of paris. *Voilà!* He'd invented a solid-body electric guitar,
the first Les Paul. Later, he turned a phone receiver into a pickup
for the guitar strings. Believe it or not, the kid built his first
recording machine in 1929, with a gramophone pickup and, he recalled many years later, the flywheel from a Cadillac. Nobody in
Waukesha, Wisconsin, had ever seen anything like it.

As a teenager, in 1930, he turned pro musician and hit the road. At one point, the wizard of Waukesha adopted the unlikely handle Rhubarb Red. Whatever the gig, for the next fifteen years, he nurtured his technical notions along with his guitar technique. Adopting the name Les Paul, the young man carved out a multifaceted career as both itinerant guitar player and intuitive technological innovator.

Famously, he designed the instrument that bears his name. Beginning in 1952, the Gibson Company's Les Paul model set a standard: these smartly designed, durable solid-body electric guitars became a favorite among players. Alongside the Fender Stratocaster, the Gibson Les Paul stands as the iconic instrument—the hallowed "axe"—of the rock god era.

A singular creation, this guitar is by no means Les Paul's sole contribution to popular music. Les Paul pioneered sound-on-sound, or multitrack, recording. Before he double-tracked his guitar lines around Mary Ford's voice on the number one pop hits "How High the Moon" (1951) and "Vaya Con Dios" (1956), the concept of overdubbing didn't exist. The now commonplace techniques of multitracking, tape delay, echo, phasing, and recording at different speeds were conceived in a garage, specifically, at 1514 North Curson Avenue in Hollywood.

Working with Fred Waring & His Pennsylvanians in the years 1938 to 1940 and gigging with his Les Paul Trio on the side, Les Paul meanwhile continued to tinker with his homemade recorders. Hooking up with Bing Crosby turned out to be mutually beneficial. Les accompanied Crosby on his 1945 number one hit "It's Been a Long, Long Time." At that point, Les had already converted his carport into a sonic laboratory. Here he perfected a crude but effective form of overdubbing with two acetate recorders and a regulation-issue turntable. He'd lay down a rhythm track on one disc, then play guitar along with it while the second recorder ran. Switching back and forth, he could add other instrumentation and even vocals. Sound quality of course deteriorated slightly with each successive generation or dubbing, but soon enough Capitol Records would sell the results of his experiments.

Frustrated by the acetate method, Les openly coveted a confiscated German tape recorder he'd seen that year, 1945. It was the infamous Magnetophon, used for Nazi propaganda broadcasts, a reel-to-reel-to-reel (three-head) machine. The first step was to arrange a viewing for Bing Crosby. Paul's sometime boss was a kindred tape enthusiast; he used tape recordings to facilitate the syndication of his radio shows. Indeed, Bing was so enthusiastic that he immediately commissioned fifty perfect knockoffs of the German machine. The California-based Ampeg Company built them to order, and a quiet revolution had begun. Naturally, Les Paul obtained one of these machines and proceeded to fiddle with it.

Les eventually added a fourth tape head to his Ampeg 300 model, which enabled it to accommodate endless overdubbing. Sound-on-sound recording left the experimental stage; Paul marketed his multitracked records under the tag *New Sound*. Early Les Paul sides made the most of his techniques. "Lover" and "Brazil," his 1948 double A side breakout, boasted no less than six overdubbed guitars.

Patti Page blazed a similar trail around the same time, perhaps by accident. Legend has it that she overdubbed vocals on "Confess" (1948) because the backing vocalists didn't show. In time-honored fashion, Page's record company (Mercury) pitched the song as a high-tech gimmick. It worked. She seemed to be singing a duet with herself.

The novelty appeal of multitracking would dog Les Paul as well. The New Sound shtick never caught on, but the clean, layered sound of sound-on-sound recording became his trademark. It was both a blessing and a curse. He and Mary Ford (Collen Summers) enjoyed a series of hit duets in the first half of the 1950s, songs that paraded technical effects at every turn. Despite the smash popularity of "How High the Moon"—nine weeks at number one—multitracking didn't catch on until years later. Paul labored on, inventing the Les Paulverizer—a recording device attached to his guitar that allowed for a sort of live multitracking. At eighty-eight, he still plays a weekly trio gig at a Manhattan jazz club.

His vintage hits were sold as novelties and perhaps that description fits. Les Paul's technological achievements are no gimmick, however. It took a while: multitracking became widely available in the wake of Les Paul's success, but nobody knew what to do with it at first. By the end of the sixties, multitracking in rock had raised pop record production to an art. The act of recording became a vital part of the creative process.

### Dreaming in Stereo

Stereo sound brought clarity, depth, and perspective to recorded music. Two channels (sources) of recorded music simulated and stimulated both human ears. Listening to mono records on the hi-fi was like watching television with one eye closed.

The advent of stereo records and record players popularized the LP format. Stereophonic sound also gave rise to multitrack recording, electronic instruments, and eventually, purely electronic popular music. Playback—a.k.a. listening to records—was enhanced and transformed, and pop itself shape-shifted to accommodate the formulas imposed by new recording techniques. At the same time, young musicians embraced the new capabilities, turning the studio itself into an instrument.

Stereo was first marketed to audiophiles via reel-to-reel tape. In 1955, Ampex introduced a stereo reel-to-reel for the home market. Since the machines were costly, stereo was pitched as a high-end toy one owned in addition to a turntable. In the early fifties, the record companies didn't push for mass-market high fidelity and stereo sound; perhaps the battle of the speeds made them wary. How many recording formats could the marketplace accommodate? Before rock 'n' roll, the answer was uncertain. So stereo, in the form of two-headed reel-to-reel recorders, remained an enthusiasm for the elite.

Audiophiles propelled the hi-fi boom. These were the tech-adept classical music buffs, hobbyists (a quaint term for geeks) who could wire fearsome home systems and even build their own components with do-it-yourself sets from companies such as Heathkit. By 1953, there were one million mono reel-to-reel recorders in use, and the record companies began to sell prerecorded tape. After all, it was easier to put two channels of sound onto separate bands of $1/4$-inch tape than to squeeze them into the grooves of a record; but this had been done nevertheless.

Experimental research in the late thirties yielded several crude but effective forms of stereo reproduction. At the Chicago

World's Fair in 1933, the Bell Company held a binaural sound demonstration billed as "two eared listening." But the marketplace wasn't deemed ready for it at the height of the Depression. Stereo research began in earnest after the war, in a period of rising affluence. Two engineers—Alan Blumlein in the United Kingdom and Arthur Keller in the United States—arrived at the same solution at roughly the same time. The actual grooves on their stereo records contain two separate lateral tracks, or motions, running at a forty-five-degree angle. A sophisticated new needle would pick up both currents of information. The stereo record player then sends the two separate channels of electrical data to two different speakers. The human ear balances the sound, creating the center we hear as "natural." Call it the miracle of perception.

By December 1957, the first commercial stereo records were introduced; the industry agreed on a universal standard (the Westrex System), which prevented another debilitating format war. Standardization was the key to widespread acceptance of stereo; the adoption of the uniform recording curve by the Recording Industry Association of America (RIAA) insured that all records would "sound good"—that is, the same—on all record players.

As the sound quality of the first stereo releases was mixed at best, consumers adopted a wait-and-see attitude. Stereophonic records accounted for just 6 percent of total sales in December 1958, one year after their debut. Gradually, as recording quality improved, so did stereo record sales. More important, most people went out and bought new stereo record players rather than convert their old mono players. By the early 1960s, the stereo disc had silenced the reel-to-reel tape format. RCA, Columbia, and

Minnesota's 3-M Company each test-marketed a primitive form of tape cartridge in the late 1950s. Unsurprisingly, these paperback-sized boxes didn't fly.

For the music industry, the sudden proliferation of stereo players brought an onslaught of new sounds—not all of them strictly musical. That "easy listening" label turns out to be rather a misnomer.

## The Sound of Living Stereo

> Mood music is perhaps the 20th century's most authentic music, tailored exclusively for the electronic revolution. These recordings fully exploit the intended use of the hi fi and stereo as domestic appliances and with all of the environmental controls of thermostats, air conditioners, and security systems.
>
> —Joseph Lanza

The extended length of the LP and improved sound quality of hi-fi fostered the excesses of the easy listening format—including kitschy "mood music." The presence of canned pop tunes piped into offices and elevators by the Muzak Company and others created a precedent of subliminal, lulling background music outside the home. In the shopping centers and dentist offices of the sixties, background music seemed omnipresent.

Wall-to-wall fullness and sonic melodrama mark even the mellowest examples. From Mantovani to Mancini, Kostelanetz to the Ray Coniff Singers, these records utilized the full range of stereo sound so that one could display one's expensive components *tastefully.*

For devotees, there existed a strange subgenre known as the stereo-demonstration disc. Even the renowned audiophile and historian Roland Gelatt had to acknowledge the underlying absurdity. "Bizarre recordings of thunderstorms and screaming railroad trains were concocted for those to whom high-fidelity reproduction was an end in itself and not a means of musical reproduction." Accordingly, the first Audio Fidelity stereo release featured the Dukes of Dixieland on one side and "Railroad Sounds" on the flip.

The fad eventually died down, but at its peak, an album titled *Persuasive Percussion* by Enoch Light sat at number one on the *Billboard* charts for thirteen weeks in 1960. Along with its follow-up, *Provocative Percussion*, the album illustrated stereo sound with ludicrous "Ping-Pong" effects ricocheting between the speakers. According to the liner notes, "When you acquire a Command recording you will have the pleasure of hearing the ultimate in true stereo recording and you can feel that your record library has grown in stature."

Apart from the novelty appeal of such records, what really spread the popularity of stereo was miniaturization. The shrinking process began even before the introduction of transistor technology, and bookshelf speakers boomed out the full range of sound in the early sixties. By the seventies, when audio components were completely transistorized, stereo sound ruled the universe. In the boom times before the advent of home computers, the audio market represented the cutting edge of high-tech amusement.

Hardware development outpaced software. Music thus had to play catch-up with technology, and musicians struggled to master the tools suddenly available to them. In stereo, the art and science of recording became doubly complex and challenging.

## Music for Heads

> A physicist will tell you that space is allied to time, but a record producer will argue that it is closely allied to sound as well.
>
> —George Martin

Another reason why multitrack recording was delayed in the pop market is that musicians were used to playing with one another. With overdubbing, each instrument performs a discrete job. Group interplay is replaced by a method of recording with exacting precision. The ability to perfect an individual performance after the fact slowly eroded the need to have people playing together at all. No more repeated takes in the studio—mistakes were taped over, new sounds dubbed in.

Vocals benefited (or suffered) the most, as they were easiest to isolate and manipulate in the mix. By the early 1960s, a new generation of tape recorders that used three heads (compared to Les Paul's Hydra four) enabled engineers to edit or cut and paste entire sections of a song while remaining in synch with the overall tempo and melody. Records would now be put together piece by piece as well as part by part. Suddenly, recording a song from start to finish seemed unnecessary.

How many tracks can fit on the head of a pin, or a single strip of tape? The number multiplied slowly, from two to four to eight in the 1960s, then rapidly shot up to sixty-four and more today. For the current generation of musicians, the recording studio has come to be regarded as more than a resource or even the means to an end: it is now the fundamental instrument for making popular music.

Who got here first? It was those omnipresent sixties idols, the Beatles, who pioneered the use of the recording studio as musical instrument. Producer George Martin mentored the Beatles, musically and technologically, without ever getting in their way. Their historic collaboration with Martin—a young staff producer at London's EMI Records—forever blurred the distinctions between music and technology.

Before the Beatles and Martin arrived in the studio, the average pop record producer functioned as a glorified bureaucrat or high-tech baby-sitter. Empowered by the advent of stereo and multi-track recording, the producer became a master craftsman—even a musical contributor.

Immortalized by a later-period Beatles album title, the EMI studio at 43 Abbey Road already possessed a distinguished reputation; the Abbey Road studio had been a leader in recording technology since Sir Edward Elgar and the London Philharmonic inaugurated it in 1931. Classical music, alongside pop drawn from the British music hall tradition, constituted the bulk of EMI recordings until the late 1950s. After the first wave of raucous American sounds invaded England, the up-and-coming Martin was deputized to find a homegrown rock 'n' roll band. When the Liverpool-based impresario Brian Epstein brought around his new quartet one day, George Martin took the meeting.

Martin pulled brilliant ideas from his background in recorded comedy, an unlikely source of inspiration for John, Paul, George, and Ringo (until you think about it). Recording physical comedians such as Spike Milligan and Peter Sellers, Martin tried to create a picture in sound. The comedy sessions screamed for an irreverent approach as well as unusual sound effects—tape run backward, multispeed techniques, whatever came to mind. Martin would record, say, four Peter Sellers tracks in mono and then mix them in stereo. The result sounded like a dialogue between a cast of characters, all played by Sellers. This experimental spirit—not to mention underlying sense of humor—obviously struck a collective chord in the four Beatles. Martin was able to translate their raw ideas into refined sounds. The fact that he read music and they didn't is only part of their story. His technical fluency lifted the Beatles' sonic ambitions into another realm.

Before the Beatles, pop records rarely received the four-track treatment. Though we recall them as primitive stabs at what soon would become legendary rock, some of the Fab Four's earliest hits were missives from the cutting edge of recording. "I Want to Hold Your Hand," with its ringing, exuberant clarity, absolutely proselytized the new technology.

String sections and classical influences crept into the Beatles' music with "Yesterday" and "Eleanor Rigby." Thanks to George Martin and great melodies, they were able to pull off this symphonic move. After the Beatles retired from live performing in 1966, their creative attention turned full time to making record albums. The modern recording studio could now serve the Beatles as a creative tool, a playground and a refuge from public glare.

The milestone that came next, *Sgt. Pepper's Lonely Hearts Club Band*, is more than a monumental "concept" album. The Beatles' orchestrated psychedelic opus is also a towering technological feat. *Sgt. Pepper's* stretched the capabilities of the studio, while unearthing rich new areas of exploration for rock. Unfortunately for the Beatles and George Martin, the next generation in multitrack recording (eight tracks) arrived right after *Sgt. Pepper's* was released, in 1967.

Yet in many ways, they'd already worked around it. The Beatles and George Martin expanded the capacity of four-track recording with basic tricks like recording an instrumental, then rerecording with three additional tracks on top of the initial rhythm track. Guided by Martin's experience and discipline, the Beatles indulged a childlike curiosity as they followed their collective muse in the studio. Millions of people are convinced that the result is recorded magic.

Eventually, inevitably, self-indulgence reared its head. Fittingly, the Beatles employed one of the very first eight-track recorders on *The Beatles*, the 1968 double-disc "White Album." A flood of sound and music pours from the speakers, stylistically eclectic and technically stunning; George Martin, however, thought it wanted editing, badly. The Beatles next tried to cut a "live" album, but *Let It Be* caught a band in its death throes. *Abbey Road*, the Beatles' last work with Martin, now sounds like a conscious summation of their achievements, and a fond farewell.

## "I Hear a New World"

The flip side of George Martin is Joe Meek. Martin's graceful ascendance overshadows Meek's tragic decline, and justly so. Born in 1929, Robert George Meek displayed astounding talent and drive during a brief and troubled life, making his way as a musician, engineer, producer, entrepreneur, and impresario. He also fit the profile of a misfit: (possibly) schizophrenic and (definitely) homosexual.

Meek also stands as an innovator, perhaps a key figure, in the field of sound recording. Simply put, Joe Meek made records that sound like no others. In fact, no other recordings were made in quite the same way. Joe Meek pioneered the DIY (do-it-yourself) approach to recording—he achieved high-tech (for the time) effects through rock-bottom, low-budget means.

Long before it was fashionable, Joe Meek worked at home. Located above a shop in a dreary London suburb, his apartment contained a roomful of jury-rigged equipment. Here he concocted science-fiction pop singles, corny and peculiar, perfect for transistor radio. Joe Meek productions transmit an utterly alien emotional sheen, an electronic noise that sounds somehow prescient. Meek deployed the sonic potential of what was available at the time: primitive electronics, cheesy echo effects, ear-drilling compression, distortion, delay. He also favored all sorts of unorthodox instruments such as pots and pans, pocket combs, milk bottles, and flushing toilets. Stomping feet in lieu of drums might be called his signature.

An early Meek effort—penned for the British teen idol Billy Fury—became a vehicle for Les Paul and Mary Ford. Talk about serendipity. Their cover version of "Put a Ring on My Finger" reached the U.S. Top 40 in 1958. Meek took the money and set up shop, so to speak. Let Phil Spector have his Wall of Sound; Joe Meek perfected the Curtain of Buzz.

Meek produced scores of records for various labels. He commanded an eccentric retinue of performers and protégés and contracted a sturdy backing band to supplement his studio gadgetry.

But his budding pop empire couldn't last. The fortress was built on sand.

For all its technical savvy and warped style, most of his work is worthless as music per se; it's pure kitsch. Somehow, Meek managed to run up a sizable handful of chart records in the U.K. during the first half of the 1960s. "Johnny Remember Me" by Anton Hollywood—death rock complete with ethereal voice from beyond the grave—sat on top of the U.K. pop charts for a mind-boggling fifteen weeks in 1961.

Believe it or not, two U.S. Top 10 hits of the time also bear Meek's indelible mark. "Telstar" by the Tornados (1962) deploys a cheap battery-powered keyboard in a quavering tribute to the satellite. "Have I the Right?" by the Honeycombs is a bright, simple blast of vintage Brit pop; that hand-clap beat practically slaps you in the face.

His moment was brief. Eclipsed by psychedelia, hounded by public homophobia and personal demons, Meek spiraled downward. He died in 1967 by his own hand after killing his landlady in a long-brewing altercation. His madness and his odd-duck music can be conflated into a campy joke all too easily. Joe Meek's recording methods, however, have proven to be unusually influential. The synth-pop sounds of the eighties, for example, echoed the wired, tinny intensity of Joe Meek records with an eerie precision.

## Headphone Music

In the wake of *Sgt. Pepper's*, the rock concept album stood as the prime example of technology's expansive effect on music. Convoluted compositions and electronically enhanced ambitions defined the field—or a significant patch of it—for years to come. Rather than rely on the usual studio musicians, rock bands reached out to new machines. The next technological milestone after *Sgt. Pepper's,* Pink Floyd's *Dark Side of the Moon,* owes much of its perennial success to synthesizers (electronic keyboards) and sound effects. Pink Floyd pioneered the use of prerecorded "click tracks" and "loops," manipulating tape to achieve metronome-perfect mechanized rhythms. And all of *Dark Side of the Moon's* spoken interjections and haunting audio verité bits (such as coins clinking and registers cashing on "Money") were accomplished on tape. Interestingly, these techniques resemble the very same hip-hop effects that so effectively spelled rock's doom a few years later. Could the art of sampling have originated on *the* classic rock album?

Multitracking reached its logical conclusion—or nadir—in the mid seventies, specifically on a hit album called *Tubular Bells.* The LP was one forty-nine-minute-long instrumental, stretching across both sides. It reached number three on U.S. album charts and supplied the creepy, catchy theme music for the film *The Exorcist.* Credit Mike Oldfield as overall auteur of *Tubular Bells.* He served as both musician and producer, playing all the instruments and stacking all the tracks. *Tubular Bells* works as a brilliant exercise in this multilayering technique, but it's something less than genius as music. Sir George Martin considered it a fluke, the work of a lucky amateur. The human touch was lost, replaced by scientific protocol. Production itself—the act of recording—now formed the core creative experience.

*Tubular Bells* was strongly reminiscent of earlier breakthrough novelty hits. The seductive allure of tech-generated music often begins and ends as a gimmick. The 1970s version of a ricocheting hi-fi demonstration record is that multitracked rock operetta "Bohemian Rhapsody" by Queen. Perhaps *Dark Side of the Moon* did for headphones what *Persuasive Percussion* did for stereo speakers.

By the mid seventies, for a sizable audience, enhanced sound quality represented an end in itself, just like in the fifties. But headphone music comes equipped with built-in limitations. Sometimes, a comfortably equipped cocoon can turn into a high-tech tomb.

## Snap, Crackle, and Pop

The Beatles set the pace for the late sixties music scene. The competition followed their every move, in music and technology. On some *Abbey Road* songs, for example, they used a spiffy new electronic instrument called a Moog synthesizer. Just a couple of years later, Moogs and similar synthesizers became commonplace, another tool in the rock 'n' roll band's growing electronic arsenal.

For the first half of the twentieth century, electronic music was the province of inventors and fanatics, the futurists and mad professors, the nerds and starving artists, the geeks and freaks. Electronic instruments were eminently impractical. Outside of an Alfred Hitchcock soundtrack, they just sounded weird.

*Synthesize* means to fuse or merge parts into a whole. A synthesizer combines electronic (or digital) parts to form a complete sound. The musical instruments we know as synthesizers produce sounds from an electronic source. An opposing approach (typically used by artists) uses electronics to manipulate or distort already existing sounds. After World War II and the development of magnetic recording tape, *musique concrete* came into vogue. The master of this form of avant-garde tape manipulation was the French composer Pierre Schaeffer. However esoteric, his *Symphonie Pour un Homme Seul* (1950) opened up sonic possibilities within the new format. *Musique concrete* also fulfilled the great fear of the twenties and thirties: A (tape) recording now played the role of musician.

Ten years earlier, the vanguard American composer John Cage dreamed up his *Imaginary Landscape No. 1*. This piece consisted of test-tone recordings played on variable-speed turntables. In retrospect, it reads like an eerie prediction of things to come.

It was the radio pioneer Lee DeForest who truly planted the seed of synthesizer development, when he invented the vacuum tube in 1906. The vacuum tube, or triode, is a glass blub containing electrodes that generate sound through a process called *heterodyning*. DeForest added a third element to the existing two-electrode tube used in early radio. The addition of another, weaker signal amplified the currents bouncing between the two electrodes. Vacuum tubes allowed for better radio transmission as well as amplification of sound. Vacuum tube technology powered the electronics, recording, and radio industries through half a century. In the 1960s and 1970s, transistors and integrated circuits gradually replaced tubes. Even today, vacuum tube–powered amplifiers for electric guitar are highly prized for a unique, low-tech sound.

The vacuum tube also powered one of the earliest and most enduring synthesizers—the theremin. The theremin wasn't the first electronic instrument, but it was the first to work with control and consistency. The machine was named after Dr. Leon Theremin, who was born Lev Sergeivitch Termen in pre–Soviet Russia.

Dr. Theremin, a gifted young physicist, built his device on an observation: The presence of a human body affected the sounds emitted by vacuum tubes. Practically speaking, playing the theremin meant waving your hands around a portable box-and-antenna set. Theremin's grand idea was to empower would-be musicians of the future. Cut loose from the constraints of fingering a keyboard and staying in tune, now anyone could produce joyful tones—or so the ads claimed. Theremin's great invention had some constraints of its own, first and foremost of which is that not anyone can play a theremin. Intonation is crucial, and what looks like a lot of abstract hand waving actually takes a great deal of practice.

Theremin came to America in 1927, not long after patenting the theremin in Europe. The machine was displayed here on a series of concert tours, to great media attention and wondrous acclaim. He may have been a communist scientist, but Dr. Theremin was also market savvy enough to hire a succession of attractive young female accompanists. The novelty of this trailblazing device included a mystical element: A theremin concert embodied the cosmic notion of music from the ether, sensitive souls plucking unearthly suspended sounds out of thin air. In reality, these events quickly began to flummox audiences, and people never knew quite what to make of the theremin's high-pitched, swooping tones. The theremin raised a question that nagged electronic music practitioners for years: Must synthesizers merely echo or mimic traditional instruments? Why not explore "indigenous" electronic textures and colors?

Ironically, Dr. Theremin wanted to make a popular instrument out of his ethereal music machine. Ultimately, he couldn't sell American consumers on the idea of a home theremin. (Sing around the family synthesizer?) He returned to the Soviet Union in the early thirties, and by 1939, he was a political prisoner. Theremin spent three months in the Siberian Gulag before being put to work on government research—as a slave laborer. When he'd departed from the United States broke and in a hurry, he'd also left his designs with RCA; so the theremin held onto its niche. Listen for its ghostly ululations during Hitchcock's *Spellbound* (1945) as well as a slew of classic sci-fi and fifties horror flicks. RCA kept the machine on the market, introducing build-it-yourself models for the home hobbyists. Dr. Theremin surely would've approved.

Eccentric-sounding yet highly effective, the theremin resurfaced in popular music during the late 1960s (of course), as an utter original. Brian Wilson immortalized the machine on a peak-period Beach Boys song, one that equals *Sgt. Pepper's* in recording-studio technique alone. Even so, the mere mention of "Good Vibrations" conjures up a sweet, familiar whine, that outer space humming. That's how it sounds. Many baby boomers have the theremin sound branded into their brains.

A contemporary of Theremin, the Frenchman Maurice Martenot invented the Ondes Martenot in 1928. Like a sit-down version of the theremin, the Ondes Martenot involved moving the hands between string and fingerboard. More important, later models incorporated a keyboard and knobs in the same configuration as a modern synthesizer. Today, progressive rock bands such as Radiohead use this vintage synthesizer both on studio albums and in live concerts.

Portability and practicality were not considerations for the majority of early synthesizers. Back when De Forest fiddled with the first vacuum tubes, a Canadian, Thaddeus Cahill, invented something called the Telharmonium. It was 20 feet tall, 60 feet wide, and weighed 200 pounds. By the technology-obsessed 1950s, the state-of-the-art RCA synthesizer, Mark I and Mark II—first choice among truly serious electronic composers—occupied an entire room, as did its European counterpart, the Siemens Synthesizer, or "Siemens Studio for Electronic Music." Like the early computers, the RCA synthesizers were programmed with punch tape. Engineers fed these hungry beasts with paper rolls of binary code.

Composer Raymond Scott provided the manic music behind the classic Warner Brothers cartoons of the 1940s and 1950s. "Loony Tunes" and "Merrie Melodies" were his specialties. Scott also put together a succession of electronic instruments; in 1952, he obtained a patent for the Clavivox. Instead of the theremin's open oscillator, the tabletop-sized Clavivox used something more familiar: a compact keyboard with a row of knobs and buttons on the side. Deemed impractical for mass production, the Clavivox nevertheless set the standard for future synthesizers: portable is preferable, and easy to play is even better.

A young engineer named Robert Moog designed the Clavivox's circuits. Growing up in Queens, New York, Moog displayed a precocious interest in electronic music. At age fifteen, poring over *Radio & Television News*, he noticed an article that would shape his life, a guide to building your own theremin. Moog clipped the three-page guide and proceeded to do just that. His engineer father had taught him well—it worked!

A couple of years later, in 1954, Moog published an article outlining his own theremin design in the same journal. Working out of his bedroom, with some help from Dad, the Bronx High School of Science student built (and even sold) a line of theremins. While a student at Queens College and then Cornell University, Moog kept a hand in electronic music by continuing to build theremins. In the January 1961 issue of *Electronics World*, Robert Moog introduced his latest refinement of the theremin concept: the Moog "Melodia." This model was eminently portable and easy to play: the Melodia weighed 8 pounds and mounted on a microphone stand. Moog sold around 1,000 units, and his theremin business was off and running.

In 1967, he formed the R. A. Moog Company and started using the term *synthesizer* to describe his post-theremin inventions: voltage-controlled modular systems using keyboards and buttons. Two years later, Moog Synthesizers could be heard on rock 'n' roll records by the Beatles, the Rolling Stones, the Byrds, and, yes, the Monkees.

It was a classical album, however, that delivered accessible electronic music to the masses. *Switched-on Bach*, an LP of classical pieces demurely performed on the Moog by Walter (later Wendy) Carlos, violated commercial convention and hit the pop Top 10 in 1969. Hearing these ultrafamiliar melodies makes the electronic context sound less alien, more human. Immediately following the success of *Switched-on Bach* came a flood of imitations and Moog novelty records. The next generation of synthesizers thus coincided with rock's growing sonic grandeur—or to some, its subsequent grandiosity.

Companies such as ARP and Roland took some of Moog's prototypes and turned them into affordable mass-market machines. He followed up with the popular Mini-Moog in the seventies, but the onset of sampling and digital synthesizers later in the decade eventually overshadowed his efforts and by the 1980s, the Moog went the way of the theremin.

At the turn of the twenty-first century, Robert Moog resurfaced with a new music machine—or rather, a new take on another old music machine. The Van Koevering Interactive Piano, developed by Moog and entrepreneur David Van Koevering, is nothing less (or more) than a digitally enhanced player piano. "There has been a very long trend away from music as a social activity," Moog told the *New York Times* in 1999. "Before the radio and electric phonograph, people made their own music, for themselves and each other. What I see now is that, more and more, we're all in our own little boxes, using the fruits of technology to make or listen to music in isolation."

When the inventor of the modern synthesizer declares that "something basic and low-tech is missing" from music, well, he speaks from experience.

chapter 6

# LAST DANCE

The new disco music is a highly contrived super-sophisticated electronic artifact . . . a triumph of art and engineering . . . the disco sound is its own and only star.

—Albert Goldman, *Disco*

THE TERM *DISCO* COMES FROM *DISCOTHEQUE*, a club where people dance to records. *Discotheque* is derived from the French word *bibliotheque*, or library—roughly, a record collection. The first discotheques were founded in Vichy France during World War II in response to the Nazi ban on jazz. This was an underground phenomenon in a true, dangerous sense. The fad continued after the war, in the open. Paris clubs such as Whisky a Go-Go and Chez Regine catered to the in crowd, the ultrahip, chic jet set. Here music provided a backdrop, or perhaps mild stimulus, for jiggling, mingling, and drinking. But the discotheque would not be an exclusive upper-crust phenomenon for long.

The roots of disco as we know it today can be traced to a seedy former strip club in New York's Times Square district called the Peppermint Lounge. Before the Beatles invaded, way back in sleepy 1960, a dance craze called the Twist came roaring out of this unlikely venue and caught America's fancy for a year or so—and then it was over, like the bunny hops and cakewalks of the past. But the movement started another turntable revolution.

As the sixties dawned, a veteran R&B singer named Hank Ballard wrote "The Twist" after witnessing the new moves being performed by teen dancers on *The Buddy Dean Show*, Baltimore's answer to *American Bandstand*. The original is a pleasantly rough bump and grind; the earthy, effective harmonies echo the lusty choruses of previous Hank Ballard & the Midnighters hits such as "Sexy Ways" and "Work With Me, Annie." Since he practically did copies of his own songs, Ballard didn't complain much when Philadelphia-based (and *American Bandstand* staple) Chubby Checker took a cover version of "The Twist" to the top of the charts in August 1960. As the rock chronicler Lillian Roxon explains, "You put one foot out and you pretend you're stubbing out a cigarette butt on the floor with the big toe. At the same time, you move your hands and body as though you're drying every inch of your back with an invisible towel. That's the Twist."

Record parties and "sock hops" were a high school ritual by the end of the fifties, but the Twist was the first widespread case of a teenage trend infecting adults. The Twist crossed over to high society. Celebrities and suburbanites alike lined up to get into the Peppermint Lounge. A group called Joey Dee & the Starlighters signed on as the house band in September 1960. A little more than a year later, they went to number one with—you guessed it—"Peppermint Twist." A few weeks earlier, Chubby Checker topped the charts *again* with "The Twist." (The only other song to do that is Crosby's version of "White Christmas.") A total of twenty-three Twist-identified singles reached the Top 40 during the early sixties: some were sublime ("Twist & Shout" was a hit for both the Isley Brothers and the Beatles), most were ridiculous ("The Alvin Twist" by the Chipmunks).

When Beatlemania struck, in 1964, the general population stopped buying cheesy Twist records and signing up for Twist instruction. Without doubt, the fad had legs. The Twist was also, as more than one pundit noted at the time, the first popular dance you did alone.

## The Big 12-Inch Record

In the smoke and shadow of the night world lived an alternate breed of disc jockey. Ironically, at the height of hippiedom, these DJs plugged into popular music's primal function—dancing. A new breed of amusement palace had begun to emerge, a place where dancing to records wasn't a sideshow but rather the main event. And the DJ ruled as musical ringmaster. Leave your preconceptions at the door and enter the disco era.

Disco is the pure musical expression of the phonograph. Generated by DJs in response to dancers, it represents the first pop-music style born and bred at the turntable. Disco began as an underground cult in New York City and developed into a definitive—and divisive—cultural phenomenon in the late seventies. Though it can fairly be labeled a fad, disco permanently changed popular music: not only how it sounds, but also how it's recorded, marketed, and consumed.

Rhythm rose to rule over melody. The recording studio and its producers and engineers came to dominate the creative process.

Sonic manipulation in the studio became an end in itself, rather than a means of reproducing the sound of a live performance. In a discotheque, the reproduction of sound is a live performance.

The ongoing reign of electronically generated music—the endlessly repetitive programs, tape loops, synthesizers, and drum machines pulsing all around us—properly begins in the disco era. Disco returned the turntable to the public sphere, and the result was perhaps the ultimate dance craze. At discotheques from Studio 54 on down, the spotlight focus of celebrity shifted from performer to audience. The mode of enjoyment switched from passive to participatory, from sitting and listening to getting up and dancing. Disco represents the last stand of a certain kind of mass hysteria.

The disco DJs reinvented pop music by taking the existing technology and stretching it a bit. The pitch-adjustment setting on the Technics 1200SL turntable—the DJ's choice—permitted minute variations on the speed of a spinning record. This allowed for smooth segues—the beat of one song merging into the next, and so on. Still, juggling a batch of 45s in front of a dance floor had to be a tightrope walk; dancers demanded longer songs and losing momentum spelled DJ death. Eventually, a new record format arose to meet the DJs' (and dancers') exacting requirements. Cobbled together from existing 45 rpm and LP formats, the 12-inch single, or disco mix, was their ungainly spawn. However inelegant, the new format worked like a charm for DJs: 12-inch singles were not only longer, they sounded better—more dynamic—thanks to the wider grooves. For consumers it would be another story—a record format that fell flat.

Just as disco came to the forefront, the sixties rock revolution flagged. The popularity of black music—the emergent disco

Thomas Edison with his first phonograph: 1877.

*Photograph by Matthew Brady*

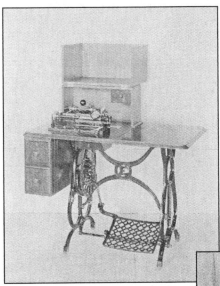

The first Edison cylinder phonograph: the Wizard's favorite invention.

*Edison National Historic Site*

Edison Phonograph Company, new releases card for July 1903.

*Edison National Historic Site*

FORM N°404-JULY 1903

NEW EDISON MOULDED RECORDS

NATIONAL PHONOGRAPH COMPANY.
NEW YORK    ORANGE, N.J.    SAN FRANCISCO
83 CHAMBERS ST    U.S.A.    933 MARKET ST.
CHICAGO    32 REMPART ST GEORGES
304 WABASH AVE.    ANTWERP BELGIUM

Emil Berliner with a model of his first gramophone: the original turntable. Undated photo.

*Library of Congress*

Peter C. Goldmark (left), director of Engineering, Research and Development for Columbia Broadcasting System (CBS), at work in the lab. Undated photo.

*Bettmann/CORBIS*

A recording format, and record player, for every member of the family: 33, 45, & 78, 1949.

American Bandstand, 1961:
"It's got a good beat and you can dance to it."

Eccentric producer Joe Meek at work in
his living-room recording studio, early 1960s.

*Hulton Archive/Getty Images*

Chicago's Comiskey Park, July 12, 1979: "Disco Sucks!"

*Bettmann/CORBIS*

Grandmaster Flash: "so nice with his hands he don't need no band."

*Photo by Laura Levine*

Afrika Bambaataa: master DJ and founder of the mighty Zulu Nation.

*Photo by Laura Levine*

Rosemary Wilson loads an Elvis 8 track into her new
RCA 12P600FM combo player.

*Bettmann/CORBIS*

February 13, 2001: Napster co-founder Shawn Fanning
reacts to ruling by the 9th District Court of Appeals
in San Francisco.

*CORBIS*

sound and Philly soul—reasserted the pop single format as an air-play medium and a unit of public consumption, if not a consumer item. Albums still ruled in record stores: singles accounted for less than 8 percent of the market in 1975. Musically, the next big thing was bubbling under the surface; buyers were restless, clamoring for something new. Eventually, the record companies would de-duce a way to sell it—or would they? Unfortunately, a classic case of overnight success clouded disco's long-term implications for the music business.

Intoxicated by jackpot sales figures, record companies didn't register the deeper impact and importance of disco. It was regarded as a novelty, a flash-in-the-pan that should be exploited quickly. That misperception soon became a gruesome self-fulfilling prophecy. At first, the flush of success was contagious. People suddenly "went disco." The movie *Saturday Night Fever* and its accompanying soundtrack (featuring the Bee Gees) kicked off the official fad, and the media attention paid to the famed New York nightclub Studio 54 firmly planted disco in the national con-sciousness. But its all-out promotional strategy and subsequent profits were double-edged swords: the *Saturday Night Fever* phe-nomenon also contributed to a postdisco backlash that nearly sunk several record companies and led to a massive restructuring of music business practices.

The anonymous nature of disco didn't make for recognizable stars, apart from Donna Summer or the Village People. Disco freaks asked for songs rather than singers when they perused a record shop, and they couldn't always get what they wanted. The problem was the recording format. Hungry for album sales—where the profit margins were bigger—the big labels never pushed 12-inch singles in a major way. Disco mixes were hard to find. Retailers accused big record companies of taking "hot" 12-inch singles off the market to juice album sales. But disco albums, which contained shortened versions of the hits along with eight or nine cuts of filler, supremely frustrated buyers, who wanted the long versions they heard in clubs. To them, paying $3.98 for a great full-length song was getting maximum value, while spending $8.98 on a mediocre LP was a rip-off.

If today that argument sounds vaguely familiar, it should. Disco was a premonition of things to come, a fad that foretold the future.

Disco didn't replace vinyl records and rock 'n' roll, but it did expose their growing obsolescence. Spurred by the success of *Saturday Night Fever*, the disco fad revived the flagging fortunes of the music business. That flush period barely lasted a year, however, and by 1979, disco took the blame for the biggest record-sales slump since the Great Depression. Still, records and record players would never again sound the same.

## Riding the Rhythm

During the mid 1960s, Beatlemania and the Top 40's glory days distracted teenage attention from the dance club scene. (The British invasion launched yet another wave of hit cover versions, while the originals languished.) Then the psychedelic hippie era moved rock's locus back to live performance; thousands of kids would sit in stoned silence watching Eric Clapton's fingers tremble. But as (white) rock soared into the stratosphere, black popular music never lost its earthbound footing or its syncopated beat. James Brown brought rhythm to the foreground in his music, distilling the essence of soul and R&B into *funk*. When he declared

"Papa's Got a Brand New Bag," in 1965, Brown outlined a bold new approach: pulsating bass and drums led the beat, stabbing horn charts punctuated gut-bucket vocals that exhorted the listener with grunts and groans, and scratchy guitar chords doubled as extra percussion.

Funk turned the sixties into the seventies. Motown musicians laid down diabolical grooves on their finest sides, and a former radio DJ named Sylvester Stewart merged funk's unforgiving rhythms with flowery psychedelic rock during the brief, brilliant heyday of Sly and the Family Stone. But it was James Brown who drew up a blueprint for the next decade of music. He was consistent and prolific, to the point of being relentless. Brown created a sound that was so technically precise and emotionally exacting and demanded such drive and discipline from his musicians that the next step had to be total mechanization.

A hero in the black community, James Brown also enjoyed a fair amount of pop airplay and crossover sales in the early seventies, but it was on the dance floor where his music made the most sense. In big cities, particularly New York, the disco scene had mutated into a new beast. While the Woodstock Nation joined hands and chanted, a fervent cult audience was congregating in New York City for a different type of communion. The true believers would gather—at small clubs, "juice bars," loft spaces, or private parties—for a taste of real alternative culture. A mix of blacks, whites, and Latinos, the mostly gay crowd would dance the night away to the sounds—soul, mostly—provided by a DJ spinning records. Perhaps the most infamous and influential spot was a former Baptist church rechristened The Sanctuary in gamy Hell's Kitchen. The name wasn't the only sacrilegious thing about it; Sanctuary was one of the first unabashedly gay nightclubs.

Egged on by the dancers, here the legendary DJ Francis Grasso—"the only straight guy in the place"—would push the envelope, testing the limits of the three-minute 45 rpm record and those of the turntable itself (in fact, he had two). Grasso's improvised solutions and innovations would help shape the next twenty-five years of popular music.

Several years before Francis Grasso, in the mid to late 1960s, a DJ named Terry Noel began exploring the possibilities of two turntables and subliminal audience participation. Noel had been a Twist dancer at the Peppermint Lounge, then became DJ at a mid sixties hot spot called Arthur. Spinning records in between live sets by a cover band, he would mix soul and rock hits with obscure personal favorites. The goal was to reach a crescendo and ride it home. "I felt up the audience," Noel would recall years later, in the disco seventies. "There's a feeling the crowd emanates like an unconscious grapevine. They send you a signal and you talk back to them through records. When I played a record, the record that followed would make a comment on the record that came before." Working two turntables with a quick hand on the volume fader was the way to do it. Only a dexterous DJ could pull it off.

Francis Grasso was the master. The Brooklyn-born DJ took this spontaneous approach and turned it into a science. Actually, the technique began in radio; Grasso perfected and patented *slip-cueing*. While one disc was playing for the crowd, he would listen to the next selection on headphones and find the best spot to make a jump. Then he'd hold still the second disc with his thumb while the turntable whirled beneath, insulated by a felt pad. At the right moment, he'd release the next song precisely on the beat. These perfect segues became a trademark, and once he got speed controls on his Thorens turntables, Grasso could alter the records' tempos so they'd match perfectly. Reaching a fevered crescendo, he'd even play two records simultaneously for two minutes at a stretch—on the same beat. Or he'd spin two copies of the same record at once, creating echo effects.

Musically, Francis Grasso's tastes were also on the cutting edge, and custom-fit for the dance floor. He specialized in soul and rock's pulsing, percussive wing, mixing Santana's steamy "Soul Sacrifice" with such African-flavored exotica as "Drums of Passion" by Babatunde Olatunji. Grasso was a maven—the original DJ with challenging taste. He played what he liked and made dancers love it.

## The Mix

> The mix starts at a certain place, builds, teases, builds again and picks up on the other side. The break is the high point. It's like asking someone a question, repeating and repeating it, waiting for an answer—and then giving the answer. That is the great satisfying moment.
>
> —DJ Danae, 1979

The disco DJs fashioned a new sound and sensibility—a nascent pop music style—that couldn't be heard on the radio; not yet, anyway. Gradually, a few "breakout" songs from the disco scene began to infiltrate the mainstream. One of the first was "Soul Makoosa" by the Cameroon-born saxophonist Manu Dibango. Hypnotic in its effect, "Soul Makoosa" relied on a chanted vocal hook ("mama-koo mama-sa mama-koo-ma-koo-sa MAMAKOOSA") and complex, compelling rhythmic repetitions. It was more than a novelty:

it was the kind of dance record you'd remember the morning after. Recorded in Paris, "Soul Makoosa" was discovered as an import by club DJs and eventually rereleased by Atlantic Records in 1973. When it crept into the Top 40 that summer, not even disco cultists realized it was an omen.

It wasn't only the music played in discos that slipped into the mainstream; the turntable strategies and rhythmic tricks of the DJs themselves began to influence the act of recording. Tom Moulton is the man who shepherded this process. He's the master of the 12-inch mix, or *remix*. Ironically, perhaps tellingly, he was never a club DJ.

A former model, Moulton pioneered the process of restructuring a record to suit the dance floor, juggling the elements of multitrack recording in order to shift emphasis. He discovered his metier while programming homemade party tapes for a Long Island disco. Turning pro, Moulton found ways to extend a three-minute song to more than six minutes by stretching instrumental sections. Working with sixteeen- or twenty-four-track master tapes, slicing and dicing, he could play up the bass and drums or whatever elements triggered a response in dancers. "A monotonous piece with few breaks or melodic hooks could be reconstructed in such a way that you lengthened the breaks," Moulton patiently explained, "or incorporated catchy tunes at the right places. Behind this was the idea to produce the best possible relation between tension and relaxation."

Merging with the producers Tony Bongiovi and Meco Menardo, Moulton utilized his ideas on a series of midseventies singles and albums by the soul singer Gloria Gaynor. Working with the original "disco diva," the team brought the New York club sound to mainstream middle America. One of Gaynor's specialties was a showstopping fifteen-minute medley in which she'd smoothly progress from song to song, flowing from "Never Can Say Goodbye" to "Reach Out I'll Be There" and leaping from "Casanova Brown" to "How High the Moon." The flow progressed with the same seamless motion a disco DJ would strive for. It was a radical move on a record album.

As the 1970s wore on, more records were made with dancing in mind, and the pop singles chart started to reflect this new trend. The Florida-based label TK Records and its light-soul "Sound of Miami" yielded Top 10 smashes by George McCrae ("Rock Your Baby") and Gwen McRae ("Rocking Chair") in 1974, and a string of irresistibly silly-sexy hits by KC & the Sunshine Band. All these songs featured swaying Caribbean-influenced rhythms and a gentle, hedonistic vibe—and they sold as well. "Rock Your Baby" was a hit around the world, selling two million here and one million in the United Kingdom. A silly piece of syncopated fluff, Van McCoy's "The Hustle" sold ten million copies in two years. Disco was knocking on the door.

## Fever

A hot disco mix . . . is a sexual metaphor. The DJ plays with the audience's emotions pleasing and teasing in a crescendo of feeling. The break is the climax.

—Andrew Kopkind, "Dialectics of Disco"

The record that finally did it, that pushed disco into the American mainstream, was all break—actually one long, extended climax. Sex already suffused popular music in general and R&B in particular. Barry White, for instance, was hugely influential, both in terms of his orchestrated rhythm tracks and his salacious, velvet-voiced come-ons.

But it was Donna Summer who would forever unite disco with the idea of mechanical sexiness. Blatant, anonymous, somewhat impersonal, and maybe even self-directed, "Love to Love You Baby" broke the field wide open, especially in its epic, extended, seventeen-minute disco version. The sultry, disembodied voice of Donna Summer shudders and sighs in orgasmic release while the syncopated backing moves through grand symphonic orchestrations and cool synthesized drones. This combination of frank sexuality and futuristic, electronically enhanced music defined a new genre: Eurodisco. When a shortened version of "Love to Love You Baby" reached the Top 10 in late 1975, *Time* magazine tagged it as the centerpiece of an alarming new movement, sex rock.

The Boston-born Summer had been trained as a gospel singer, toured Europe in productions of *Hair* and *Godspell*, and in Berlin had hooked up with the producer Giorgio Moroder and his songwriting partner, Pete Bellotte. They sculpted a fresh sound for her: rhythm-driven, with room for melody and ambition to spare. Suites and concept albums were the stuff of Eurodisco. Other producer–artists such as Cerrone and Alec Costandinis took this approach even further on their own albums: Eurodisco's shimmering technological edge and stiff robotic beats complimented the science-fiction fad of the late seventies and paved the way for the mechanical, purely synthesized sound of the eighties.

"We take something from everything," Moroder declared, "and then we make it our own."

Disco is soon to be the R&B sound of today. [In 1978, that wasn't obvious.] And these ideas that writers are having about using machines and becoming like machines—they must be making a joke. I know for sure we are, and maybe, as I think you say in English, we are having the last, longest laugh. All this talk of machines and industry makes me laugh. Even if you use synthesizers and sequencers and drum machines, you have to set them up, to choose exactly what you are going to make them do. It's nonsense to say that we make all our music automatically.

Perhaps the mechanical nature of disco has been overemphasized—or indeed, demonized. With its relentless repetition and studied anonymity, disco feels like a self-aware celebration of mass production. Is this truly such a threat? The vast majority of pop songs and singers are faceless and interchangeable; cover versions and copycat artists go all the way back to the beginning of recording, when every record company worth its wax released a rendition of "After the Ball." The history of pop music is an endless scroll of one-offs, overnight sensations, hypes, disposable idols, comic novelties, and sentimental favorites. A final word: *Nobody* got the last laugh on disco.

## The Crash of '79

Then we went to Studio 54. Truman was there. He goes up into the crow's nest where the DJ spins the records and it's like his private office. People come up to see him, and he stays until 8:00 . . . Rod and Alana were in the back, I introduced them to the manager. It's hard to get coke there now, they're not really selling it.

—Andy Warhol, *Diaries*, Saturday, January 6, 1979

We will have more *Saturday Night Fever*'s and great years, but the lessons of 1979 will not be forgotten. "Profitless prosperity" is a term we could do without.

—Barrie Bergman,
president of Record Bar retail chain, 1979

The communal ecstasy and high style of the urban disco scene spread to the suburbs, gradually sweeping middle America via two concurrent tornadoes. The movie *Saturday Night Fever* and its accompanying soundtrack launched the disco craze, and the media's obsession with celebrity-studded Studio 54 defined disco in the national consciousness. The brainchild of Long Island restaurateur Steve Rubell and his partner, Ian Schraeger, Studio 54 epitomized the decadent image of disco. It was aggressively exclusive, ambitiously elegant, and unabashedly gay. During its heyday, from 1977 to 1979, "Studio" made a star of everybody on the dance floor—that is, anybody who could gain admittance. Drug and tax evasion convictions closed the club in 1979 and both owners spent time in jail. They weren't the only disco entrepreneurs who suffered through rough mornings after.

If disco was producers' music, then *Saturday Night Fever* was a producer's film. The bond between the movie and songs on the soundtrack album set the stage for many a marketing package to come. The complex, enveloping web of tie-ins and synergy starts with *Saturday Night Fever* (and *Star Wars* as well) in 1977.

The producer Robert Stigwood assembled the *Saturday Night Fever* package after reading and obtaining the rights to a 1976

*New York* magazine article portraying restless postteens in a Brooklyn disco, "Rituals of the New Saturday Night," by Nik Cohn. Stigwood had a background in movie and theatrical production (*Jesus Christ Superstar*); conveniently, he was also manager of the Bee Gees. Comprised of the three Gibb brothers (*Bee Gee* stands for brothers Gibb), this Australian pop group made their name as sweetly harmonizing Beatles clones in the late 1960s. After a fallow period, they'd reinvented themselves with vaguely funky dance hits such as 1974's "Jive Talkin'." In the film, a white-suited, open-shirted John Travolta made the dance floor seem accessible to blue-collar youth; the pumping music and suavely choreographed dance scenes levitated the corny, follow-your-dreams plot. And the soundtrack album was cleverly split between the Bee Gees' satiny, sanitized grooves and compelling, authentic disco classics such as the Trammps' "Disco Inferno." *Saturday Night Fever* perfectly defined a musical movement, and millions of middle Americans couldn't resist hustling on board. Undeservedly, perhaps, the Bee Gees were recast as disco's blow-dried Chubby Checkers.

Of course, one sequence from the film will live forever in pop's collective unconscious: John Travolta in his white suit, looking magnetic, *dancing by himself.* Disco was a solo turn by definition, albeit performed in a group setting. The sublimated sexual motion of an old-fashioned teenage slow dance would be utterly superfluous in a modern 1970s discotheque.

Eventually selling more than thirty million copies, the *Saturday Night Fever* album spent twenty-four weeks at number one in 1977 and 1978. The marketing campaign, masterminded by veteran record man Al Coury, connected like none previous. In December 1977, half a million copies of *Saturday Night Fever* shipped all at once. Movie trailers that prominently featured songs were shown in theaters, a prime example of crossover marketing. Four singles were released simultaneously, and each wound up in the Top 10 at the same time (equaling the Beatles' British invasion coup). Yet these record companies soon would come to rue this kind of oversaturation.

At first, the flush of success was contagious. Explains WBLS DJ Frankie Crocker in 1979, "Disco is definitely replacing rock . . . rock is no more important than Dixieland jazz in New York City right now." Nationwide chains of *Saturday Night Fever*–style nightclubs opened. Radio stations adopted disco formats—reluctantly. Before the bust, ads for a line of Studio 54 blue jeans appeared. A Broadway musical titled *Got Tu Go Disco*, budgeted at half a million 1979 dollars, mercifully went belly-up. Recording artists lined up to remake themselves as dance mavens. Some of these conversions were suspect, to say the least. Rod Stewart, the Beach Boys, Cher, Dolly Parton, Shirley Bassey, Andy Williams, Barbra Streisand, Englebert Humperdinck, Helen Reddy, Herbie Mann, and Ethel Merman all released nominal disco records. Country veteran Porter Wagonner announced (or was it a threat?) that he might record a disco version of "The Star-Spangled Banner." Somehow the quacking "Disco Duck" sold four million copies, but most of these unlikely crossover hits bombed. The campy carrying-on of the costumed Village People —however charming in their self-deprecating humor—became synonymous with disco itself. Their success branded the genre a musical joke. And no matter how funny it is, any joke has a severely limited shelf life.

The Roman-candle flameout of Casablanca Records, the home of Donna Summer, the Village People, and KISS dramatically illuminates the commercial crash-and-burn of disco itself. Casablanca's founder, the late Neil Bogart, rode the rocket; in his time, he had become disco's reigning mogul.

Bogart (née Bogatz) was a consummate striver. Prescient enough to sign Donna Summer after hearing "Love to Love You Baby" in Europe, Bogart insisted on releasing the radically long version of the song. He also instituted the play-fast-and-loose business strategy that eventually spelled doom for disco. Still, those giddying highs must've had breathtaking peaks. At first, the numbers surely were intoxicating. In 1978, Bogart's Casablanca and Stigwood's RSO combined sold $300 million worth of records for the joint owner, Germany's Polygram.

Bogart's career path began in Philadelphia, at the Cameo-Parkway label; his connection to Dick Clark and the Philly teen-idol scene runs deep. He honed his chops at Buddah Records, the late sixties home of bubblegum music. Buddah's preteen pop is an eerie prediction of disco in some ways: conceived by producers and studio musicians, assigned to bland or anonymous performers, relentlessly promoted.

Before disco, the foundation of Bogart's empire was built on the cartoon-rock of Kiss, the loony funk of Parliament, and a flukey LP of *Tonight Show* comedy routines. Not surprisingly, Donna Summer's breakout success saved Casablanca from crumbling. Doubling its bet on disco, the German conglomerate Polygram purchased a half stake in Casablanca in 1977. (Polygram had owned a piece of RSO since 1975.) The influx of money, however, only served to justify the questionable practices at Casablanca.

One favored Bogart ploy was overshipping—that is, sending out many more copies of a record than the market demanded, logging them as sales and notching up another platinum hit. The only problem was in returns: since there was no limit on the number of unsold records a store could send back for a full refund, retailers would accept any size shipment.

The Casablanca roster included the Village People, but the label also signed dozens of other artists whose records, in the words of one ex-employee, "shipped gold and returned platinum." On top of general overspending and mismanagement, amid rumors of rampant drug use, Bogart made gigantic miscalculations that undermined even his surefire successes. Releasing four solo albums by members of Kiss in 1979 didn't exactly turn the tide. Casablanca went under a few years later, an overdose victim of disco-era indulgence.

Casablanca was merely the most extreme example. All of the major labels had an overly generous return policy until 1979, the year they got burned. According to historian Russell Sanjek, "CBS and Warner had spent in excess of $20 million to erect new manufacturing facilities in order to meet expected large sales. Finding themselves, instead, with millions of LP returns, they lowered the boom on the 100% return policy. There was also the problem of counterfeit LPs among the returns." In the wake of *Saturday Night Fever*, record sales hit a slippery slope.

The death knell of disco sounded during the summer of 1979. The funeral rites occurred in a baseball stadium on July 12. A popular Chicago radio DJ named Steve Dahl staged an ominous promotional event at Comiskey Park in between games of a White Sox doubleheader. It was a publicity stunt gone haywire and a bitter expression of the growing divide in popular music. The unified musical discourse of the 1960s splintered into a shrill, unnecessary debate: rock versus disco.

This so-called Disco Demolition started with Dahl blowing up an enormous pile of disco records in center field. Dressed in military garb, the DJ fled in a jeep before thousands of his fans stormed the field. They destroyed signs, tore up the sod, knocked over the batting cage, and caused the second game to be canceled. A fairly recent arrival at rock station WLUP-FM, Dahl was protesting his former employer's (WDAI-FM) move to a disco format. He was also pandering to the rabid "disco sucks" mentality that had invaded the pop music scene—or at least the male adolescent end of it. Homophobic and obnoxious, to be sure, this small-scale riot also reflected a widespread ambivalence toward disco in the general population—an ambivalence rapidly curdling into outright hostility. Like any musical fad accelerated by mass media, disco had saturated its audience and worn out its welcome. The backlash had begun, and it was brutal.

Yet the Chicago antidisco rabble probably didn't appreciate the full irony of their publicity-grabbing protest. Their funeral pyre burned not just for disco; the LP format itself was on its last legs. Both cassette and compact disc were waiting in the wings. Before those struggles could begin, however, the phonograph had to complete its journey from playback device to musical instrument, from record player to turntable. Luckily, the next generation of radical DJs emerged from the unlikeliest of places just in time. Hip-hop would pick up the thread exactly where disco left off.

## chapter 7

# ADVENTURES ON WHEELS OF STEEL

THE INCREDIBLE HIP-HOP SAGA actually begins on an island even more hardscrabble than the Bronx—Jamaica. In the 1950s, long before the rise of reggae and the Jamaican music industry, sound systems, or mobile discos, dominated the island scene. Live bands were mostly limited to the tourist trade. Speakers, amplifier, and a turntable mounted on the back of a truck met the basic requirement, though anyone equipped with rare R&B records from the States gained status. Massive volume was also key—especially fat, pumped-up bass lines that could rumble through dancing crowds.

The sound system operator, or DJ, functioned as both technician and selector, requiring an equal mastery of technology and music. The most successful sound system operators—Duke Reid, Sir Coxsone, Prince Buster, and King Tubby—eventually started to cut records by local acts. So they morphed into entrepreneurs, by necessity, becoming DJs in the Dick Clark sense. Gradually, a uniquely Jamaican variant of R&B known as *ska* issued forth from sound systems. In time, the local music scene grew into something deeper, ever more singular and complex. Ska turned into reggae as its bass lines grew even fatter, peppy horn charts receded, and the creed of Rastafarianism surfaced in the lyrics.

Even as the music played on these sound systems developed into something more indigenous and original, however, the DJs, or operators, continued to manipulate or distort the records to their own ends: boosting the bass and volume, conjuring spaced-out special effects, adding verbal commentary and between-songs patter. Verbal introductions, announcements, segues, and slang could be supplied by a sidekick, also known as a DJ, or toaster. Scatting and exhortations in the singular island patois became a crucial ingredient in the sound system mix; by the turn of the 1970s, toasters such as U-Roy became recording stars in their own right.

The toaster sputtered commentary on the passing parade like a stoned carnival barker. The background for his spiel was often the borrowed rhythm of a popular record. Literally, anything was fair game. The *version* (as in cover version) came to rule Jamaican music, mostly because the field was wide open—until 1993, Jamaica had no copyright law pertaining to music. You didn't have to pay to play or make records; a Jamaican cover version didn't cost a penny. Such legal concepts as plagiarism and piracy had no meaning. The British critic Dick Hebdige supplied a hindsight label for this new kind of music making: *cut 'n' mix*. No one owns a song or melody or rhythm; music makers simply borrow tunes, returning them in slightly different form.

Roughly at the same time, in the mid sixties, both Coxsone and Duke Reid started to make their own records. Laboring in Kingston's handful of recording studios, they laid the groundwork for reggae's world takeover. Working in his Studio One (the first black-owned studio in Kingston), Coxsone over time established the fundamental methods of record mixing. Obscure but crucial is that in addition to his famous efforts with Bob Marley and countless others, Coxsone cut hundreds of one-off party discs. These were specialized records born of need and tailored specifically for the dance floor. Made on the cheap and not originally intended for commercial consumption, they were rough analogues of the 12-inch single—test runs for the next revolution in sound recording. Even more than the disco mix, the *dub plate* was malleable, open-ended raw meat for the DJ.

The dub plate was usually a 10-inch acetate. Think of these clunky discs as stepping-stones, as formative pauses on the way to the finished product. Dub plates introduce the idea of an *unfinished* record, recasting pop music as a work in progress (for the technologically capable). Perhaps the science of record mixing begins with the dub plate.

Working with just two tracks, the sound system engineer took songs and pared them to a basic rhythm piece—just drums and bass, with most of original vocals removed. Songs then could be refit with different singers or lyrics and preexisting rhythms fit with different songs. One song could be slightly reshuffled and rerecorded in fifty (minutely) different versions for fifty different sound systems. The variations were fluid and forever multiplying. By the late 1970s, a track known as the Real Rock Rhythm was reputed to exist in 800 versions (including "Armagiddeon Time" by The Clash).

One day at Duke Reid's studio, in 1967 or 1968, a happy accident changed the course of Jamaican music (and also prefigured some of disco's innovations). A sound system operator, Rudolph "Ruddy" Redwood, happened to hear a tape on which the engineer forgot to add the vocals and liked the eerie quality of the instrumental version. Ruddy asked Duke to put it on the back of a record and took it to the dance that night, and a new sound was born—*dub*. The instrumental version was more than a flip (or B) side: it was raw (or half-cooked) wax, a template; successive singles could be cut from the same backing track, or rhythm.

The key figure in dub history—a sound system DJ tinker turned scientist, Lee "Scratch" Perry—cast a mad shadow over reggae. Working in his homemade studio, Black Ark (a backyard setup), Perry broke new ground during the 1970s. He deployed his crude recording equipment willfully, using its defects and shortcomings as sound effects. Perry embodies the transforming power of technological innovation utterly on the cheap. In his homemade studio, Perry concocted sounds and techniques—a whole recording aesthetic—that others still employ, at far more expense.

Overdubs, abrupt silences, an abundance of echo and distortion, and ghostly, half-spoken and chanted vocal snatches drift through the throbbing mix. Lee Perry produced legitimate hit records, for all his signature bizarre qualities. Two of reggae's crossover classics bear his stamp: Max Romeo ("War Ina Babylon") and Junior Murvin ("Police & Thieves"). And his early seventies alliance with Bob Marley was a formative collaboration for both. Perry produced the Wailers on some key 1970 sessions, subtly guiding them from U.S. R&B toward a topical Jamaican roots sound. Scratch's midseventies deal with Island Records gained the dub sound some international exposure during reggae's commercial heyday.

Dub paved the way for dancehall in the 1980s; the wake of Bob Marley's death spelled retreat for reggae culture at large. Naturally, Jamaican music returned to the sound system at that point, only to be revived and refreshed as dancehall a few years later. If the staccato fire of Jamaican dancehall—liquid verbal dexterity and mechanical rhythms—resembles American hip-hop, this is because there is indeed a direct connection.

## The Holy Trinity of Hip-Hop

The Bronx was already home to a sizable community of Caribbean immigrants in the 1960s and 1970s, but the musical connection between reggae and rap can be traced to one man. Clive Campbell, better known as Kool DJ Herc, moved to New York at age twelve in 1967. Growing up in Kingston, Campbell had been exposed to the sound systems at an early age (that is, he was too young to actually attend the dances). When he began to spin records himself, at parties in the early 1970s, he naturally emulated that approach. The reggae records he played at first didn't spark the same response in New York, so Herc (as in Hercules) developed a new repertoire, heavy on James Brown and funky soul with Latin percussion from local favorites such as Mandrill and The Jimmy Castor Bunch.

Like the disco DJs, Herc employed two turntables to insure nonstop dance floor action. Where Francis Grasso developed smooth, beat-perfect segues, however, Herc deployed abrupt, attention-grabbing transitions. He noticed that certain sections of records—usually percussive breaks or isolated beats—always elicited a strong response from his audiences. So why not give the people what they want? Spinning on two turntables allowed Herc to cut to the chase, literally. With two copies of the same record, he could play one section over and over, returning the needle to start one record while the other played through. Thus he could extend a record's peak indefinitely, working the crowd into a frenzy. The term for his manual edits became *break beats*.

Herc labeled his raucous adolescent (mostly male) audience the B (for *break*) boys. Their ballet of hyperathletic moves on the dance floor morphed into the art of break dancing, and their calligraphic art—spray-paint graffiti of Byzantine complexity—could be seen everywhere in the city, thanks to the mobile canvas of mass transit. Hip-hop culture was born.

Hip-hop started as a black bohemian movement, like bebop, only younger and farther uptown, in the Bronx. If the DJs resembled jazz soloists in flight, then the early rappers snapped and stretched the sounds of their words like scat singers. Hip-hop arose from recording technology, a pure product of the turntable. In turn, the new music sparked the next generation of changes in that industry. After hip-hop, records would never be made the same way again. To put it bluntly, a lot of professional musicians lost their jobs.

Hip-hop didn't have time for disco's tension and release, all those anthem choruses broken by extended vamp sections. As the British observer David Toop succinctly put it, "Break-beat music simply ate the cherry off the top of the cake and threw the rest away."

Continuing another tradition of Jamaican DJs, Kool DJ Herc relied on a powerful sound system and became known for punishing levels of bass emanating from his own "legendary" speaker cabinets (the "Herc-U-Lords"). Initially, Herc handled MC duties himself, pausing between songs to add encouragement—a Bronx-accented slant on the slangy rhetoric of the toaster. "To the beat y'all, you don't stop"; "Rock on, my mellow."

As his fame spread, Herc recruited a pair of MCs—Clark Kent and Coke La Rock (*sic*)—and played dances in public parks as well as local hangouts such as the Hevalo, Disco Fever, Executive Playhouse, and Twilight Zone. There were other DJs around at the time, such as Pete "DJ" Jones, Grandmaster Flowers, and DJ Hollywood, but Kool Herc commanded a hardcore following. Between his jump cuts and exclusive taste for hard funk, Herc's sound ruled the streets—until two younger men came along. Grandmaster Flash and Afrika Bambaataa took Kool Herc's break-beat approach, refined his technique, and broadened its appeal. They brought hip-hop to the world at large.

Growing up in the South Bronx, most boys couldn't afford a bedroom sound system. Young Joseph Saddler developed the knack for repairing disabled equipment, assembling a homemade rig from the ample refuse surrounding him. Between his technical expertise and fascination with his father's record collection, the future Grandmaster was a natural on the turntables. The aspiring DJ Flash improvised his own variation on Herc's style—and improved on it. Hitting the streets, literally, Flash conducted market research at ad-hoc dance parties in the local concrete-and-trees parks. Power source: a jury-rigged telephone pole, more often than not.

Perhaps not as stridently antidisco as Herc, Flash favored hard-driving funk beats but he'd also pull romantic R&B harmony records from his crates as the night wore into day or vice versa. Flash prided himself on the breadth of his record collection and the length of his DJ performances. He never had to repeat himself by playing the same record twice.

According to Flash, Herc didn't seem quite comfortable with headphones and his mixes sounded crude as a result: he'd drop the needle by eyeballing the record grooves. Flash made maximum use of headphones, precisely mixing one record into another and experimenting with the process. He'd augment the record while it was spinning, switching the mixer from his headphones to the speakers for isolated blasts of sound, adding an emphatic brass riff or drum slap. He called it *punch phasing*. Eventually, he devised a way of using the record itself as a percussion instrument. This procedure—quickly moving the record back and forth over the same beat or chord—became known as *scratching*. Flash makes it seem simple.

Actually, Flash modestly defers full credit for the scratching technique. He cites the influence of another DJ, his boyhood friend and neighbor, Theodore Livingston, a.k.a. Grand Wizard Theodore. Too young to spin records at parties, Theodore advanced the DJ's science behind closed doors in his bedroom. When his mother yelled "turn it DOWN" one fateful day, he held the stylus while the record kept spinning. "What Theodore would do with a scratch is make it more rhythmical," said Flash in 1993. "He had a way of rhythmically taking a scratch and making that shit sound *musical*. He just took it to another level." That resulting sound—*wicka wicka wick*—is now recognized as the hip-hop DJ's sonic signifier.

Herbie Hancock's "Rockit" (1983) propelled the scratch technique into the pop eye, courtesy of one Grandmixer DST. This hit single and early MTV staple is also (for its time) a high-tech fusion of break beats and synth blips. The rhythmic skips and hops of live DJ scratching had never appeared on a pop record before—"the freak crossover success of 1983," noted *Rolling Stone* magazine. "Rockit" also furnished the background for a million television sports events through the years. The scratch has been a recurring note in pop music ever since, for some, an annoying noise that won't go away.

If Flash (and Theodore) advanced hip-hop as a science, then Afrika Bambaataa pushed the new form forward to a broader culture. A former member of the Black Spades gang, Bambaataa led the transition from street crime to street creativity. He founded the Zulu Nation, a peaceable crew dedicated to hip-hop with the same organization and fervor that the gangs had devoted to drugs and violence. Devoted to the philosophy of "James Brown, Sly Stone and Louis Farrakhan," these Zulus were far more tolerant and inclusive than many of their Nation of Islam brethren. (Their name was inspired by *Zulu*, a 1966 film featuring Michael Caine and some stunning technicolor battle scenes.)

As a DJ, Bambaataa's taste was marvelously eclectic. "I played so much crazy shit they called me Master of Records." Hardcore funk and break beats were both his base and springboard. He'd play the Beatles *and* the Monkees, hard rock by Grand Funk Railroad and Thin Lizzy, the theme music from the Pink Panther cartoons—any record with a rhythmic break or catchy hook was game. Behind the turntables, Bambaataa wasn't a technical whiz in the engineering sense, as Flash was. He'd even allow his acolytes (Jazzy Jay and Red Alert) to physically implement his selection. Years later, even Kool Herc admitted that Bambaataa "could turn my head around" with offbeat choices—a catholic taste was Bambaataa's secret weapon. To prevent espionage, he'd disguise the labels on his discs.

Bambaataa and Flash, like Herc before them, attracted devoted followings among teenagers in the Bronx. Gradually, word spread throughout the five boroughs of New York City. Cassette tapes of DJs were circulated and car services and private taxis would obtain a "dope" Herc, Flash, or Bambaataa tape in order to attract and maintain customers. And as this music grew in complexity and sophistication, the role of the MC, or rapper, increased. Grandmaster Flash led the way in this arena as well. His first sidekick was Cowboy (Keith Wiggins), who wielded the deep, mellifluous voice of a radio announcer. Cowboy gets credit for introducing rhymes into hip-hop's verbal mix. Next to join Flash were the Glover brothers, Melvin and Nathaniel, better known respectively as Melle Mel and Kid Creole. They brought a literate, hyperarticulate spin to the proceedings. With the addition of Rahiem (Guy Williams) and Scorpio (Eddie Morris), the crew became known as Grandmaster Flash and the Furious Five. They were unabashed showmen, rapping in unison and individually, playing their vocal cords and vocabularies like percussion instruments, incorporating homemade costumes and Temptations-style dance routines into their act. But the driving force behind it all, and perhaps the center of attention, was the action behind the turntables.

In 1993, Kool Herc said he shrugged off the prospect of recording. "I was always maintained as far as running the sound system and giving parties. The Mic was always open for the MCs. My thing was just playing music and giving parties. I wasn't interested in making no records." Eventually, the rappers caught the ears of the people who make the records. At that point, on records, hip-hop turned into rap. Yet that great leap forward took a while.

Grandmaster Flash and the Furious Five were the obvious candidates to put hip-hop onto records. But how could you make a record of music based on other records? Others were interested, of course, yet these originators weren't the first. Like Bill Haley in the early days of rock 'n' roll, the first true rap record didn't come straight from the source. Sylvia Robinson, the coowner of Sugar Hill Records, first heard the sound of hip-hop from her children and threw her considerable business acumen behind it. Rap music, as it became known, put this street-smart, black-owned independent label on the map. Robinson assembled a group called the Sugar Hill Gang. Basically a trio of wannabe rappers, they borrowed rhymes from established Bronx stylists, most notably Grandmaster Caz of the Cold Crush Brothers. The Gang's "Rapper's Delight" crossed over to the pop charts in 1979, mostly on the strength of musical hooks lifted from Chic's late-disco hit "Good Times." That ascending bass line and liquid pulse were repeated in a hypnotizing loop while the rappers plied their rhymes. Chic insisted on a royalty payment, naturally. Sugar Hill settled and set another precedent.

Sugar Hill Records finessed the problem of how to record DJ music with help from an expert crew of studio musicians. They appropriated beats and subtly recast melodies, reshuffling and polishing until their borrowings sounded shiny and new, or at least novel. If that sounds like an approximation of the DJ's approach, it should. After recording for the even smaller Enjoy label, Grandmaster Flash and the Furious Five signed with Sugar Hill and released a succession of sleek, exciting singles. "Freedom," "Birthday Party," and "It's Nasty (Genius of Love)" function as party chants and also feature fearsome levels of verbal dexterity and an irrepressible love of language.

Despite the endless verbal tributes paid to Grandmaster Flash on all of the Furious Five's classic raps, the king of the quick mix is strangely inactive on these early records. "I wasn't ready," Flash said of making records; by the standards of that time, he was right.

Those standards were upended, however, with the 1981 release of "The Adventures of Grandmaster Flash on the Wheels of Steel." A showcase of the DJ's mixing talents, "Wheels of Steel" features bits of "Good Times," "Another One Bites the Dust" by Queen, "Rapture" by Blondie and more, topped off by voiceovers, drum breaks, and the rough, percussive *wicka-wicka-wick* of scratching. Then and now, *Wheels of Steel* sounds like nothing else on earth: the first record made entirely out of other records. "I wanted to do something like ["Wheels of Steel"] for a long time," said Sylvia Robinson, in 1981. With perfect hindsight, she continued, "I spoke to Flash about it and he said, 'A record? Are you serious?' The kids really like doing that on turntables. It took about a day to do directly from record to tape. Flash is really the best."

Sugar Hill no doubt aimed "Wheels of Steel" as a novelty, but this cut-and-mix milestone presaged the day, soon to come, when records could be made without the services of any musicians, or any traditional musician at least, save a vocalist or two. Once again, the record business was undergoing subtle changes that would ultimately lead to a major transition in how music would be recorded and produced.

The next 12-inch single by Grandmaster Flash and the Furious Five, "The Message," had a more immediate effect—thanks to the supercharged social realism of its lyrics and Melle Mel's deadpan staccato delivery. Rap would no longer be party music. Yet the terse synthesizer figure at the center of "The Message" turned out to be as influential as the so-called message itself. Electronic sounds came to dominate pop in the mid 1980s, and black pop (R&B as well as rap) provided both the blueprints and the proving ground.

## Die Mensch Maschine

> In a simultaneous exchange, rap music has made its mark on advanced technology and technology has profoundly changed the sound of black music.
>
> —Tricia Rose, *Black Noise*

Released around the same time as "The Message," another early rap single energized the eighties. "Planet Rock" by Afrika Bambaataa & Soul Sonic Force solidified the live-wire connection between black music and technological innovation. "Planet Rock" became a left-field commercial sensation, the only certified gold 12-inch single of 1982. Soul Sonic Force's rhymes and lyrics are weak compared with the Furious Five's output, and their message, aside from the music, is nonexistent. But the haunting synthesizer echoes and eerie machine beats of "Planet Rock" heralded a new methodology of recording. Processed by the hip-hop DJ, tweaked and rewired, the clockwork mechanical repetitions and hypnotic synthesizer drones of Kraftwerk somehow re-emerged as dance music.

Kraftwerk took technology to heart. More accurately, Kraftwerk took technology *as* its heart. Kraftwerk is the pulsing embodiment of purely synthetized music, generated by a new race, *die mensch maschine*. *The Man Machine* is not only the name of a Kraftwerk LP but also defined the group's image and methodology. Group leaders Ralf Hutter and Florian Schneider created a sonic template composed of layers of synthesized textures overlapping precise beats. Of course, Kraftwerk acknowledged the human role by mocking it outright.

Kraftwerk's 1975 opus "Autobahn" ambulates for more than twenty minutes, filling one entire side of an LP record. Such indulgences were common at the time, but *Autobahn* stretched the album format subtly out of proportion. The serene synthesizer ebb and flow subverts the limits of the LP, along with the listener's sense of time. Every so often, oceanic waves of human (Beach Boys) harmony roll through the window. Compatible with American expressways, the *Autobahn* album hit number five here in the States. Almost as a teaser or perverse joke, an edited 45 rpm version even floated into the Top 40.

Kraftwerk's "Trans Europe Express" reached a different audience, by accident or design. In retrospect, what attracted Bambaataa is obvious. Underneath the immaculate layers of keyboard sounds, the mechanical rhythms nail down a groove. On the *Trans Europe Express* album, the travelogue title track segues neatly into the resonant ricochet of "Metal on Metal." Interestingly, it took a crew of Germans to replicate break beats. Even the hiphop DJs were awed. Grandmaster Flash confessed to putting Kraftwerk on the turntable and letting it spin, unedited. Shifting tracks such as "Trans Europe Express" and "Metal on Metal" didn't require further cuts.

## The Music Machine

Eventually, technology caught up with the DJs. In the recording studio, keyboards and samplers made handier tools than two turntables and an endless stack of records of records. In time, a supplement to the DJ's turntables became a substitute.

The expansion of the hip-hop DJ's palette began with the beat box. The first drum machines literally were beat *boxes*, preprogrammed analogue machines that let you choose a basic rhythm pattern. A crude metronome pulse functioned as the hook on George McCrae's "Rock Your Baby" and "Why Can't We Live Together" by Timmy Thomas, two key entries in the Miami Sound predisco sweep. Grandmaster Flash blazed this side trail, supplementing his rig with a dinosaur beat box (made by Vox). While Flash approved of this supplement to the turntables, he consistently resisted the use of samplers in the 1980s and 1990s. So the recorded rap revolution left Flash behind. He still spins in New York clubs and on the radio.

Afrika Bambaataa, though, immersed himself in the new technology of the early 1980s. Along with the producer Arthur Baker, Bambaataa relied on the services of John Robie, a keyboard player and, more important, a programmer. On "Planet Rock," the soon-to-be ubiquitous Roland 808 drum machine provides the pulse. A Fairlight sampling keyboard regularly emits a polyphonic *blat*—the compressed reproduction of ten orchestras squatting on one note. This neck-snapping hook worked every time, becoming one of many thunderous 1980s dance music clichés. Thankfully, the technology that produced these inhuman sounds was capable of generating more humane sounds as well.

Reproducing them in recognizable form led to legal problems. A copyright skirmish erupted over "Planet Rock," this time between Kraftwerk and Bambaataa's label, Tommy Boy Records. According to Tommy Boy founder Tom Silverman, his pioneering rap and dance company had to pay dearly for the inspiration. From the first, another precedent was set: dance to the music, pay the piper. Eventually, record companies realized that paying DJs to actually *play* the new machines would be cheaper than paying royalties for every direct quote or appropriation. Still, pay to play remains the name of the sampling game. Hip-hop is purely functional music. The DJs aren't disrupting the past with their mixes and cuts; rather, they're putting it to use.

Rap crossed over into the (white) mainstream in the mid eighties, when Run-DMC hit with a hip-hop version of Aerosmith's hard rock warhorse "Walk This Way." And the homemade techniques of hip-hop DJs crossed over too: Engineers and producers in expensive recording studios adopted the ideas behind scratching and break beats. Synthesizers, digital samplers, and drum machines could enhance the rhythmic collages generated by the turntables—or replace them outright.

Sampling became the high-tech version of DJ mixing, especially the way hip-hop DJs would "cherry pick" or take snatches of breaks, beats, and hooks from records. Sampling used digital technology to take apart and reassemble prerecorded music to give it new meaning. The development of inexpensive digital samplers, synthesizers, recorders, and computers brought the most advanced sound recording techniques within reach of the home user.

A sampler converts analog sounds (from recorded sources) into digital code, stores the code in memory, and converts the digital code into analog sound (playback). At first, due to limited memory, samplers could only supplement the DJ's turntables and records. But as technology improved, sampling gradually lured the DJ away from turntables. Programming offered a quicker and more efficient method of mixing.

The mellotron was probably the first sampler. This archaic device was a late sixties staple, often mistaken for an early synthesizer. It's the droning keyboard used by the Beatles, Led Zeppelin, Pink Floyd on *Dark Side of the Moon*, and by the Moody Blues on everything. Actually, the mellotron did function as a crude sampler, as the keyboard triggered recorded musical notes on tape loops. Typically, mellotrons were utilized to "re-create" the sounds of instruments (as opposed to creating "pure" electronic sound); as a result, the mellotron has been associated with a soupy sound usually meant to echo a string section.

Another early protosampler was the Optigan, a toy marketed from 1971 to 1975. Built by Mattel, the Optigan was an electric organ knockoff, a keyboard with sounds supplied by a locked-groove record player inside. Owners received a set of insertable 12-inch discs. The discs held recordings of organ, drums, bass, piano, guitar, and so on. Press the keys on a keyboard and a light beam would play the celluloid discs, in much the same way that a movie projector would "play" the soundtrack strip on the film.

In 1979, the Australians Peter Vogel and Kim Ryrie developed a true music-sampling machine, the Fairlight CM, a massive tabletop keyboard with a big TV monitor. By all accounts, the Fairlight produced crude sound—but it could *reproduce* anything. Also popular was the Emulator by EMU, which was similar to the Fairlight but even bulkier and less practical. Then came the funky Synclavier, a distinct-sounding digital synthesizer that added some sampling capacity. AKAI made sampling accessible to the average musician, offering short memory on affordable machines such as the iconic AKAI S–1100 sampler. These machines empowered an entire wave of British pop in the 1980s, not to mention American R&B.

Synthesizers, samplers, and drum machines became as common as the Technics twin turntables: Linn-Drums, Roland and

Oberheim, and more. Microprocessors introduced memory capacity and acoustic sounds could be stored digitally, recalled, and recombined at will. The ability to program your own rhythms while manipulating stored beats made for (seemingly) infinite variations. In modern hip-hop, the role of record spinner (DJ) has morphed into record maker (producer).

Rap music has assumed the name hip-hop once again, but turntables are no longer the prime tool in the hip-hop DJ's arsenal. The cult of the turntable has continued on the fringes of pop culture.

## Defenders of the Faith

There are still DJs who operate the turntables, creating live sound collages through athletic displays of spinning skill. The turntablists are DJ crews who raise the competitive bar of early hip-hop several notches higher. Armed with two turntables and a mixer (phaser), they channel the art and science of disc jockeying into a form of musical sport. Call what they do *analog scratching*. And the nature of their performance is decidedly athletic—a contest or "battle" such as the International Turntablist Federation World DJ Battle held in Amsterdam in late 1998, or the Technics-sponsored North American DJ Championship held in New York City in 2000.

These events are more akin to sports matches than dance parties; DJs are judged in strict categories such as scratching, beat juggling, freestyle spinning, and team routines. Prominent turntablist crews include the Incredible Scratch Pickles (Bay Area), Beat Junkies (Los Angeles), and X-ecutioners (New York

City). Other turntable tag teams scratch records throughout the American suburbs, in Europe, and of course Japan. All it takes is a stack of records and a lot of practice.

Such turntablism isn't concerned with music per se; for the most part, you can't dance to their on-the-spot sound collages. Indeed, they don't play the records so much as they play the scratch. As macho as early hip-hop could be, in the end it was all about "rocking the house." At least the turntablists don't take themselves seriously. The sense of humor is goony and obvious; to a man, these extreme DJs splice and dice bits of comedy, mostly TV and movie dialogue from the likes of rubber-faced seventies icon Jimmy "JJ" Walker.

"There's one style of DJ-ing where you can only use this once scratch," explained DJ Q Bert (Richard Quitevus).

That's the standard scratch sound. If you can mess with that sound and manipulate it in a unique way, then that gauges your skill. Then there's the other style, where you can use any sound you want.

You're really only taking sounds from other people's records and using them to make something new, and I'm only using second-long sections of those records. It's hard to explain, but I'd say it's like making a collage—a bit like taking the face of a monkey and sticking it onto the body of a giraffe in order to make a new creature.

The old-school Bronx masters have enthusiastically endorsed the turntablists as their successors. Grand Wizard Theodore is their role model, Afrika Bambaataa their spiritual godfather. But are they furthering that tradition or just preserving it in strict formalist terms? Recall that the turntable itself is a piece of outmoded hardware.

Are turntablists defenders of the faith? In a narrow sense, they're extending and reinventing hip-hop on a purely technical level; Sean "P-Diddy" Combs probably couldn't do what they do. But music itself often goes missing and is indeed missed. Too often, turntablism revolves around technological innovation and technical perfection. In other words, turntablists tend to be long on skills, short on style. And make no mistake, the original hip-hop DJs had style to spare.

Lately, the top turntable crews have been making their presence known in the mainstream. X-ecutioners significantly dented the *Billboard* pop album chart in March 2002, when their CD *Built from Scratch* debuted at number fifteen—the strongest showing for a turntable act to date. "Hopefully our success will prove we're musicians," DJ Rob Swift told the *New York Daily News*. "We're not just playing records. If you just heard it, you might think it was just samples. When you see us, that's when you know we're building it from scratch."

Once you get past the pun, the ambition of Swift's statement sinks in. In the hands of the X-ecutioners and DJ Shadow, the turntable is no different than the electric guitar. These high-tech pancake flippers didn't replace musicians, they became musicians. In effect, they joined the union. In the long run, the great fears of James Caesar Petrillo were groundless—or were they? While machines haven't yet completely replaced musicians, they certainly have replaced more than a few musical instruments.

## chapter 8

# SUDDEN DEATH OF THE RECORD

"CDs are shit!" he said with sudden, surprising bitter-
ness. "Horrible, emasculated travesties of their analog
originals. They are nothing more than a plot concocted
by greedy record companies to gull brainless consumers
into discarding their vinyl and repurchasing the very
same performances in overpriced, sonically inferior
forms. It makes me furious to think that the medium
which has preserved some of the greatest performances
of the greatest music ever written is being sacrificed
wholly for gain. These things are priceless time machines." He tapped the album with his forefinger.

—Jonathan Valin, *The Music Lovers*

DURING THE DARKEST DAYS of the postdisco depression, a tiny
light flickered at the end of the tunnel. When *Billboard* noted the
introduction of a new cassette tape player in the December 8,
1979, issue, the earth didn't move—at first. Described as "Sony's
Tiny Stereo Player," the Soundabout was a handheld, 14-ounce
playback-only machine that used headphones and standard-size
cassettes. Retail price: $199.99.

The future was clear, with one catch: Following this particular path would lead the music business away from the record player and the record itself. Any revolution in music technology impacts on two fronts: software and hardware. In most cases, hardware developments are harbingers of trouble among software formats.

When *Billboard* announced the arrival of the Walkman in 1979, the accompanying article also laid out some safe predictions for the ensuing decade. "Cassettes are expected to emerge as the dominant form of prerecorded tape by early next year." Yet the following caveat seems overcautious in retrospect, that "no one is predicting the early demise of the 8-track form." In fact, 8-track tapes disappeared in the next three years. By 1983, prerecorded cassette sales caught up with vinyl record sales, but the record industry hadn't even begun to fight. The cassette battle was a mere skirmish, a contained conflict that eventually triggered the mother of all format wars.

Records and record players, of course, were not suddenly declared obsolete; they became obsolescent, and slowly but surely they grew less useful as objects, at least to the nonobsessed listener. Maintaining a large record collection tends to get in the way of daily life. At a certain point, all those albums begin to take up space. You can really fill a room with shelves, cases, stacks, racks, and entire walls of classic albums, platters du jour, trifling vinyl cupcakes, and timeless desert-island discs alike. The reality is that not only do records accumulate, they're also more or less immobile. Listening to records is largely a stationary activity.

The cassette tape challenge crept up on the record industry, quietly gaining ground in the postdisco chaos. Perversely and perhaps fittingly, the advent of the cassette tape comes roughly 100 years after Edison's groundbreaking 1877 invention. In 1979, annual sales of audio products were neatly split between three formats, with $2.1 billion worth of vinyl disks sold, along with $1 billion in prerecorded cassette tapes and $1 billion in 8-track tapes. Yet few if any industry pundits guessed that cassette sales would overtake vinyl records in the 1980s. Eight-track tape was the first obstacle for cassettes to overcome.

Today, the 8-track format is fondly recalled as a relic of smiley face seventies kitsch, about as practical as a pair of men's platform shoes. Conceived by William Lear, inventor of the Lear Jet, the 8-track cartridge contains a continuous-loop tape with four sets of paired stereo tracks. Beginning in 1966, the Ford Motor Company installed Motorola 8-track players in its cars as a luxury option. In an exclusive software deal, RCA offered hundreds of prerecorded selections for the new machines to play back. The success of the 8-track format (by 1975, it accounted for 25 percent of all prerecorded music sales) must be attributed to the automobile. Convenient for drivers owing to its size and shape, an 8-track tape could be inserted and removed with one hand while driving. Tellingly, this awkward format never caught on outside the car-crazed United States.

In hindsight, the obvious shortcomings of the 8-track format negate any of its virtues. Despite a generous total playing time of one hour, the 8-track tape automatically switched from one pair of stereo tracks to the next, which means glaring interruptions in the middle of a song. Also, a selection couldn't be repeated without running through the entire tape. There was no fast forward or rewind, which meant 8-track tapes didn't manually cue as a cassette did; and while the sound quality of 8-tracks couldn't compare to vinyl LPs, it sure beat cassettes, at least for the time being. With the advent of Dolby noise reduction that advantage gradually eroded.

Compact-sized cassettes were portable as well, and not only when installed in the dashboard of a car. The handheld transistor radio of the sixties was replaced in the seventies by the boom box, or ghetto blaster, named in honor of its marketplace. These hulking rectangular compacts—including radio, cassette player, and a pair of speakers in one machine—could be carried like a suitcase or hoisted onto an ample pair of shoulders. For the young, mobility was important and the turntable came to be seen as a cumbersome stationary object. Record players were still the centerpiece of any serious sound system, but the alternatives to owning a turntable were multiplying, sounding better, and dropping in price. In the expert hands of a DJ, such as the radio jocks of the sixties or the disco and hip-hop innovators of the seventies, turntables fueled public consumption of pop music.

Portable cassette players, though, fueled private consumption of music. Headphones became ubiquitous on urban streets. It is no accident that the new generation of players in the early eighties became known as *personal stereos*. Almost overnight, portability turned into a crucial issue for audio consumers. People now expected freedom of movement while playing back prerecorded music—or at least they demanded it as an option.

By 1981, Sony's aforementioned Soundabout had morphed into the Walkman II, a model that was 25 percent smaller than its predecessor and contained 50 percent fewer moving parts—and it was cheaper too. Other manufacturers followed Sony's lead, and the same trademark name, *Walkman*, stuck. It became generic, applicable to all personal cassette players, like the Victrola eighty years earlier. The Walkperson's reliance on headphones—unlike the all too conspicuous consumption of the boom box fan or car stereo buff—intensified a new dynamic, the one-on-one experience of music and portability: immediate and intimate, purely individual, and somewhat isolating. By 1989, Sony had sold twenty-five million of its various Walkman models in the United States. By that time, overall U.S. sales of personal stereos hit twenty-five million units per year. The move toward the personal stereo clearly indicated where audio technology was heading, which was away from the turntable. Sales of vinyl records plummeted during the 1980s. The popularity and portability of cassette players undoubtedly had much to do with this decline. In 1981, roughly 100 million prerecorded cassettes were sold, and 308 million LPs; the next year's figures were 125 million and 273 million, respectively. By 1986, the numbers flipped, with 350 million cassettes sold versus 110 million LPs.

Despite the overall rise in the combined sales of prerecorded tapes and discs, the music business decided that consumption of blank tape was eating away their profits. As Russell Sanjek noted at the time, while CBS's music sales hit $1 billion in 1979, operating profits dropped almost by half. Forty million buyers of blank tape made a handy scapegoat—or target. In 1980, a CBS study reckoned that home taping cost the industry hundreds of millions of dollars and then the die was cast. Clearly, home taping represented a greater threat than any competing technology. The record industry responded with the ugly and hugely unsuccessful Home Taping Is Killing Music campaign.

The RIAA and its members claimed that home recording was a form of piracy and began lobbying for a tax on both tape recorders and blank tape. For the most part, their efforts were too little and too late. By the early 1980s, tape recording had become simple; the only skill required was being able to push a button. A random sampling of any home music collection would've turned up homemade tapes. Still, the massive success of Michael Jackson's *Thriller*, coming as it did at the height of the home taping controversy, didn't exactly bolster the record industry's empty-pockets argument. Nor did an independent study by the Copyright Royalty Tribunal, released that same year. The results indicated that home tapers purchased the most recorded music and possessed the deepest pocketbooks. How could it be that affluent consumers with large appetites were murdering the music business? In retrospect, the entire controversy reads like shtick: "Business is good, but these home tapers are *killing* me!" Confronted with a new format, record makers looked at a potential ally and perceived an enemy. It wouldn't be the first time that the music industry resisted technological change rather than turn it to a positive (that is, profitable) end.

Now, of course, it seems perfectly logical, elemental: Home tapers would continue to buy records. What else would they tape, without commercial interruptions? For most consumers, home-programmed cassettes served as an accompaniment to records—enhancement, not replacement. Perhaps the deeper threat behind home taping was this implicit act of consumer empowerment, the ability to select; and indeed a deadly threat was exactly what the record industry made of the cassette trade. Home taping gave listeners the power to program. Call it freedom of choice.

Records were in a rut. Home taping offered an escape from all those crappy LPs. By 1980, there was an actual physical glut of vinyl. Hit records stayed in the market longer, while tighter return policies strangled small record stores. A flood of cutout LPs (discounted and nonreturnable) helped to sink some retailers. Inevitably, prerecorded cassette sales began to dent LP sales. The ruling format had sprung a leak. And the ensuing furor over home taping exposed a fatal flaw in records.

Cassette tape recorders always held that promise of freedom of selection. You could play DJ, in a sense. Japanese manufacturers began adding cassette players to hi-fi systems in the early 1970s. The smaller tapes were easier to handle at home, and more important, they could be used for recording as well as playback. Inexpensive stereos with turntable, radio, and cassette player empowered the average listener: Now you could tape a copy of almost anything you heard. For a while in the mid 1970s, FM radio facilitated home taping with midnight "album hours." Indeed, many stations would actually broadcast a tone so that everyone could set their meters accordingly. Aside from portability, the cassette format promulgated as well a crude form of interactivity. Armed with reasonably priced technology, consumers could now compile, program, and package their own albums.

In the end, cassettes remain sonically inferior (arguably) and less durable (surely) than vinyl records. Cassettes deteriorate quickly, and often get chewed up during playback. But one advantage of cassette tapes over records is that they don't scratch or skip. This may have been their initial strong point. Moreover, the LP format had been compromised, mortally wounded during the music industry's postdisco slump. Another revolution hovered in the wings, in the form of a dramatic new sound technology and playback-only format. Digital recording and the compact disc would launch the ultimate format war.

Let's digress for a moment. The parallel between videotape and audiotape is imprecise but interesting. The film industry fought against the advent of the videocassette recorder (VCR) for a while in the early 1980s, briefly insisting that videotapes be purchased and kept instead of rented and returned to the store. That effort failed, and Hollywood quickly realized that watching movies at home and buying tickets at a movie theater were complimentary, not competitive, activities. As with music, the so-called threat of video home taping was relatively small potatoes. It became a joke, since nobody knows how to program a VCR in the first place.

Whether video technology or music technology, commercial success in the mass market is obtained via mastery of hardware through standardization and domination of software through availability.

Consider the case of a failed hardware format called *quadrophonic sound*. This four-channel "double stereo" sound system of the early seventies was doomed from the get-go. Lack of standardization inflamed a confusing, hypercompetitive situation: Companies brought out stereos and released records that were incompatible with one another. Appeal to consumers was apparently not even a consideration. Adding to the mess, availability was inconsistent at best. The number of "quad" record releases was severely limited, as major labels hesitated to choose any one delivery system. The sonic advantage of listening to four speakers at once was unclear as well, and the quadrophonic revolution was over before it even began.

In the videotape format war, Sony lost a similar battle. Sony's Betamax format was the first technically successful VCR when it debuted in 1975. It soon was wiped out by the competing VHS system, even though Betamax came first and was generally regarded as a higher-quality machine. It was reminiscent of Edison's fight, when his cylinder phonograph came up against the disc-playing Victrola. Not only did VHS tapes run slightly longer, many more movies were available on VHS than on Betamax, and in the end, user choice was key. If Sony had had access to a film library, it might have been different. As it was, Betamax went the way of quadrophonic sound—straight to the consumer-electronics junkyard.

Akio Morita, cofounder of Sony, ultimately accepted responsibility for the fatal Betamax decision. The VHS format emerged as a viable alternative because Sony had refused to license its technology to other Japanese electronics companies. The competition joined forces, thereby guaranteeing that VHS would rise as the dominant format.

Sony wouldn't make the same mistake again. In 1988, they bought CBS Records for $2 billion. As a leading manufacturer of compact disc players, Sony now had the software—a music catalogue, including Michael Jackson—to sell alongside its hardware.

## Zeros and Ones

Digital communication was born in the telephone labs. In fact, the dot-dash system of Samuel Morse's telegraph can be seen as a crude approximation of binary code, which is the basis of digital sound and digital computers. Digital sound works through the pulse-coded modulation (PCM) of audio signals into digital code. This process transmits an enormous, dynamic range of sounds with little or no background noise.

Perhaps a brief review will clarify this complex progression. Edison's acoustic phonograph mechanically reproduced sound waves, shaping them in the soft wax of the cylinder. Electrical recording, the next step, converted sound waves into varying voltages of current; they could then be reconverted to wave form in the record's grooves, or stored on magnetic tape. Finally, digital recording turns the sound waves into a pulsating electric current that can be measured and expressed as a binary code of digits.

In 1978, the Netherlands' Phillips NV wheeled out a prototype compact disc player comparable to today's players, but it played slightly smaller discs (4.5 mm) compared with today's CD norm. Having learned a lesson from the Betamax debacle, soon afterward Phillips and Sony teamed up for a standardized—and hence universal—compact disc format, agreeing to produce compatible machines and software. Sony's experience with the Walkman guaranteed portability; Phillips had manufactured cassette cartridges since the early 1960s.

The first commercial compact discs were offered for sale in 1982. Right away, the differences between vinyl records and the new format were dramatic. On CD, the clarity and definition of sound are certainly noticeable. The absence of background noise means that every instrument in the mix comes through loud and clear; fullness takes on new meaning.

Instead of splicing and dicing tape, digital editors alter binary code. It's possible to make hundreds of changes in a few seconds of music: surface noise, blurs, muffling, pops, and clicks can all be eliminated. Older, predigital (analog) recordings could also be converted to digital with little discernable difference. This allowed a wealth of music to be heard—and purchased—by a new, presumably hungry, audience. If the improved quality of digital recording and remixing sounded clinical and dry to some, many more perceived the new format as a revelation.

The compact disc's advantages don't stop at sound quality. CDs run nearly twice as long as conventional forty-minute LPs— seventy-four minutes and forty-two seconds, to be precise. As far as the compact disc itself goes, size mattered (in reverse). The compact disc's 5-inch (12 cm) diameter made CDs easier to handle and carry. Improved portability enhanced the appeal of a CD—perhaps it could replace both LPs and cassettes. Prerecorded CDs are intended for playback only, of course, but they are programmable: you can hear songs in the sequence or duration you choose. While slight damage is done each time a vinyl record or cassette tape is played, the CD does not suffer similar deterioration (or so it was claimed). Unlike the diamond stylus of a turntable, the laser on a CD player doesn't wear or tear the disc as it reads the encoded sounds. Theoretically, a CD will last forever and sound the same every time it spins. No warps, stretches, scratches, or skips: not from playback, anyway. Handling them is a different story.

Compact disc sales started slowly, then hit their stride just as cassettes became the dominant format. In 1986, when cassettes led at 350 million units sold and album sales dropped to 110 million units, about 50 million CDs were sold. Two years later, compact discs outsold vinyl for the first time. During the preceding ten years, between 1978 and 1988, LP sales had dropped 80 percent even as the overall music market grew. Singles sales had fallen off the map; the 45 rpm record became the province of radio DJs and jukebox operators. The conversion movement gathered steam quickly.

Compare the first six months of 1988 with the first six months of 1989: Compact discs sold 70.4 million copies versus 43.4 million LPs in 1988, and 96.8 million CDs versus 17.5 million LPs in the same period one year later. During the first five months of 1989, 1.2 million CD players as opposed to a mere 180,000 turntables were sold. By 1990, an estimated 90 million turntables were still in use across America. One nagging question remained. How often did consumers actually use them? One possible answer is not as often as they might've wished, because there weren't as many new records as there used to be.

## CD Versus LP: Victory by Any Means Necessary

The transition from turntable to CD player proceeded quickly, but not fast enough to suit the music business. Though the movement to digital clearly was unstoppable, the record industry gave it a firm shove in the years 1990–91. Rather than fade away, records were removed from record stores. Almost overnight, CDs replaced LPs and vinyl albums were relegated to back shelves, cutout bins, and bargain basements.

The major record retail chains—Tower, Camelot, Sam Goody, Coconuts—took a proactive approach. Sensing the shift, they chose to anticipate customers' changing preferences rather than play catch-up after the fact. In 1987, a small and ambitious reissue label, Rhino Records, born in the back room of a store in West Los Angeles, launched an unsuccessful campaign to save the LP. Four years later, Rhino had no vinyl releases scheduled. "The problem with LPs is we couldn't make any money selling them," said Harold Bronson, Rhino's managing director. By late 1990, most of the aforementioned chains either had dropped or severely reduced the availability of vinyl. Mom-and-pop specialty stores soon became the only well-stocked vinyl outlets. "Nobody is buying them," declared Russ Solomon, president of Tower Records. "So why sell them?"

That wasn't a problem with CDs, at least not for record companies. New CDs sold for $15 or $16 compared to $9 or $10 for LPs. Even as the manufacturing costs of CDs equaled and eventually fell below the cost of making records, their retail price stayed the same. Overall growth slowed in the music business during the early nineties, but profits were high because CDs cost more. The reissue phenomenon further fueled this prosperity; catalogue sales blossomed as consumers replaced their scratched-up vinyl collections with crisp, clean CD reissues. Eventually, this bear market had to fade; as the boxed-set memorials multiplied, record company vaults were plundered. Ironically, Rhino Records—once denigrated as a novelty-obsessed oldies label—cleaned up on this trend by licensing catalogue rights from major labels and releasing a seemingly endless stream of retrospectives and compilations. Yet the reissue boom created a backlash in a sizable group of wary, cynical consumers who were in no hurry to replace their "permanent" CD collections with yet another generation of software. The latest format war ended in short-term victory for the music business, but companies paid a long-term price for their profits.

From the start, retailers questioned the new arrangement. In the LP to CD shuffle of product, the feeling was plain: record stores were getting screwed. There were a few lone cries in the wilderness that went largely unheeded. One such clarion came from the very top of the chain. Investor Stanley P. Gold, whose Shamrock Holdings company owned the Music Plus chain and other record stores at the time, administered a bracing wake-up call in 1990. Addressing a music-biz convention, Gold chided a roomful of major record company executives by branding them an "oligarchy" that willfully inflated prices. Quite reasonably, Gold suggested lowering the wholesale price on CDs from roughly $10 to $7. The record industry consortium disputed his numbers, but Gold insisted that the cost of manufacturing a CD had dropped from $2.50 to $1.25.

Sporadic grass-roots resistance flared. For a few months in 1990, the owner of a Virginia record store named David Campbell defied the high price of CDs. He contended that record companies could sell three times as many CDs at a price comparable to prerecorded cassettes. Campbell's noble and dramatic gesture made a point but didn't leave a lasting mark. This brave soul became the Don Quixote of the CD pricing scandal, an unlikely hero tilting at a high-tech windmill.

In 1989, Campbell bought a 30,000 CD inventory for his store, The Music Man, in a Norfolk shopping mall. "They just sat there," he told *Newsweek*. "It nearly put me out of business." So Campbell lowered his "front line" CD prices to $11.98 (from the usual $15.98 or $16.98). Campbell claimed that his monthly sales more than tripled—rising from $19,500 to $70,000. Of course, his margin was so low that he lost money and eventually had to raise prices again—but not before he took out a full-page advertisement in *Billboard* in 1990, challenging the music industry to follow his lead and cut prices. The national media jumped on Campbell's story, but the record companies patiently waited for him to come around, along with everybody else. Campbell's experience wasn't unique, but this particular grass-roots rebellion never got off the ground. Records were disappearing. Forget availability; compact discs achieved *inevitability*. CDs surely won the format war against LPs, but it was a victory achieved through a cunning stealth campaign.

Obviously, popular music also changed in ways that accelerated the CD revolution. The divisive effects of disco had split the world into self-sufficient, mutually exclusive spheres by the 1980s. Fragmentation became the buzzword, as every style, subgenre, and splinter group had its own support system. MTV and music videos overshadowed radio and hit singles, making television the means of dissemination for each new generation of fans. MTV's initial reluctance to broadcast videos by black artists—the last gasp of FM radio's "disco sucks" backlash—sparked a controversy in the early eighties. That fire had to be cooled by the network, because CBS threatened to pull all its videos if the door didn't open—and the rest is history. Michael Jackson waltzed on through, pointing the way back to a color-blind crossover (in pop music, anyway). Ten years later, middle America was conquered by a constantly broadcast stream of hip-hop videos from both urban coasts.

## Death of the CD?

Technology is moving at such a fast pace now I wonder if another five years something might begin to replace the CD. I can see the total demise of software in the future. You'd have a system where every song ever recorded is on a central computer, and people would subscribe to a service where they could punch in the song they wanted on their stereo and it would play it.
—Jim Mayhercy, Last Chance Records (Chicago), 1990

Prerecorded music has two dying configurations—cassettes and singles—while the mainstay configuration, the CD, is more than twenty years old. You can't expect growth from the configuration scenario.

—John Marmaduke, Hastings Entertainment, 2001

I think the CD system will be around for another 20 years. There is no reason for it to go away. Certainly not because of the Internet—which will never represent mass tonnage market for albums. It will only be good for singles or free music.

—Russ Solomon, Tower Records, 2001

The bright, expansive compact disc helped to shape the synthesized sounds of the previous two decades. One exception to this high-tech sonic juggernaut was the postpunk underground rock scene, where passion and nonconformity mattered more than production values, and vinyl records remained a viable medium. Independent labels such as SST Records—an Orange County, California, source of low-budget classics by Black Flag, Sonic Youth, the Meat Puppets, Hüsker Dü, and the Minutemen—were shrewd and economical in their cult focus. The trick consisted of releasing just the right number of records and getting them to the right listeners. A collegiate circuit of clubs guaranteed support and survival if not financial success. The so-called Indies didn't get rich, but their bohemian dedication prolonged the life of vinyl into the nineties.

Once Nirvana cracked the Top 10 in late 1991, underground rock turned into major-label grunge. At this point, the CD revolution was complete. Kurt Cobain and company's breakthrough album *Nevermind* transformed the music business like nothing since *Saturday Night Fever*. The parallels are inexact, but striking enough to merit comparison. In both cases, crossover marketing corrupted an underground-bred style, reduced it to fad status, then ran it into the ground. Just as disco inexorably led to the record slump of the late seventies, the flood of inferior grunge CDs (Nirvana knockoffs with one good song per hour-long album) nearly choked the music business in the latter half of the 1990s. Just as hot disco mixes demanded the extended 12-inch singles format, the five-minute energy blasts of grunge were best preserved on (low-tech) 7-inch vinyl singles. Nirvana's crossover and the grunge fad came too late for any possible rehabilitation of the 45. Back in 1990, a front-page story in *Billboard* diagnosed the entire singles format's health status as moribund, "in its death throes." One remaining genre of music depended on the vinyl format. Once independent-label rock got absorbed into the corporate monolith—joining forces with the compact disc revolution—fewer and fewer vinyl records indeed were even released.

In the late nineties, the seeds of disenchantment were sprouting among music consumers. People grew frustrated with the CD itself, those 3.5-inch-wide wafer-thin plastic wheels, as well as the sounds contained within.

Valiantly and in vain, Sony twice tried to vary and improve the CD format's appeal. The Pocket Discman, in 1987, was a portable playback-only machine that used 3-inch CD singles. Unsurprisingly, the CD single format tanked as both hardware and software. Record retailers rejected the CD single, and by the turn of the decade it had been replaced by the *cassingle* (cassette single). Songs were still the measure of pop currency, but to purchase them individually no longer made sense.

Initial attempts to supplement the CD with a new format were unsuccessful. Clearly, a CD-quality tape was the place to start.

Sony unveiled its digital audio tape (DAT) in 1990. DAT was half the size of a traditional cassette, playing up to three hours and rewinding in seconds. To most people's ears, DAT offers the same purity of sound as compact discs, yet there were two immediate drawbacks. The hardware price tag was heavy and software selection was thin. One year later, Phillips responded with its own digital tape format, digital compact cassette (DCC). These tapes were the same size as traditional cassettes, and they were also compatible, which meant old tapes and old tape players didn't have to be immediately discarded. Again, major flaws existed: the players were pricey and prerecorded tapes were scarce or nonexistent.

Neither format caught on with the public. Today, DAT is widely used in recording studios. For obvious reasons, record companies fiercely opposed digital home taping in the early nineties and the RIAA went to work, lobbying in Washington, D.C. In 1992, Congress imposed a royalty on blank digital tape, to be paid to composers, performers, and record companies. The dire threat of piracy, or home taping, was vanquished.

The MiniDisc came next. It too never quite caught on. Introduced in 1992, and marketed exclusively by Sony, MiniDiscs offered the same seventy-four-minute capacity as CDs at roughly half the size. Sony expected its MiniDisc to replace the failing cassette format and then perhaps supersede the CD itself (a mere ten years after CDs emerged). Today, in 2003, this delusional Mini-Disc mission clearly must be judged a failure. The problem is that none of the three competing formats—DAT, DCC, and Mini-Disc—are compatible with one another. Each cancels the other out.

The cassette wound down, eventually wearing out of its own accord. The portability of CDs and ease of operation made the cassette seem redundant and as clumsy as its packaging: an awkward, eminently breakable little plastic box. Cassette sales decreased every year, from 1989 on. The compact disc became the ruling format; but ubiquity has its downside. The fundamental flaw, the limitations of CDs, became apparent, at least to a far-sighted few.

By the end of 1996, CD sales growth had stalled, while many suspected that perhaps music itself had stagnated too. Several years down the road from the vinyl phaseout, Tower Records chief Russ Solomon sounds less than sanguine. "We don't have any teen idols," he mournfully noted. (A sad state of affairs that would flip in less than a year with the arrival of the imported Spice Girls.) "Record companies have been busy trying to create new technology," he continued, "like the mini-disc and the digital cassette, which have been flops, instead of focusing on music."

Moreover, those permanent, impregnable CDs certainly do scratch, skip, jump, and emit strange beeps, especially when you play them over and over. According to the bottom line–minded *Wall Street Journal*, by 2001, between $1 billion and $4 billion worth of unplayable CDs had accumulated in America's collective living rooms, assuming that a modest 1 percent damage rate translates into $1 billion worth of faulty discs. Compact discs may be more durable than vinyl records, but they sure are sensitive. A little oil from your finger can ruin that CD in a magnetic flash.

Reminiscent of the great vinyl floods of 1980, by century's end there was a CD surplus, an absolute glut. The music business's focus on blockbusters translated into a random hit-or-miss approach multiplied by platinum—that is, millions and millions of copies unsold. That time-honored show-biz practice—throwing a load of crap at the wall and waiting to see what sticks—can back-fire, despite all the technology in the modern world.

The first half of the nineties signaled a boom period during the rise of alternative rock and suburban country; the second half greeted a parade of one-hit wonders and overnight sensations of questionable durability. "Maybe we're seeing the start of a new development," said British executive Rob Dickson in 1991. "There will still be loads of hit records, but not so many actual artists." Perhaps this was a self-fulfilling prophecy; by 2003, it still feels like an accurate assessment of the pop scene.

In 1999, less that 1 percent of the myriad CD and cassette titles released sold more than 10,000 copies, according to Soundscan (a computerized sales monitor). Hence, 99 percent of new releases didn't appear on the racks of mass-merchandise stores such as Wal-Mart. Forget about the fabled mom-and-pop operators; the idea of a sizable retail store specifically devoted to music products suddenly seemed doomed.

According to a dire *Washington Post* report in 2001, the end was approaching. "Specialty chains like Tower records—which typically carry 20 times the merchandise of Wal-Mart—are steadily losing market share." The same article noted that "the typical Wal-Mart carries roughly 4,000 titles." So much for the once-vaunted catalogue sales, lifeblood of the boom; surely by now, every vinyl treasure had been traded up for the CD. At any rate, the vaults had long been emptied of everything but curios, castoffs, rehearsals, and reruns.

Even though teenage pop ruled the charts during the late 1990s, nominal grown-ups became the music industry's fastest growing group of customers. According to the RIAA, consumers over age thirty-five accounted for 35 percent of all sales in 1999.

Ten years earlier, that count was a mere 28 percent. More and more, CDs were becoming the province of baby boomers—an affluent quality-minded demographic with established tastes and buying patterns. The young must be hungering for their own format. Now, each successive subgeneration expects audio hardware and software custom-fit to suit the times. Everybody deserves a portable and affordable recorded soundtrack to (extended) adolescence—and technology continues to deliver it.

One key feature of the MiniDisc might have enticed younger consumers, had anyone paid attention. These *compact* CDs carried audio and data (text). They were also rewritable; in other words, you could erase and rerecord music while maintaining digital quality. MiniDiscs were a resounding dud, but they nudged open a door that couldn't be easily shut. Sony and Phillips reunited and developed a rewritable CD in 1989. In time, commercially marketed prerecorded CD-ROM discs featured elaborate audio and visual display for home computers, but the audio mode was invariably playback-only.

Though rock survived the millennium, the rock album showed signs of formal burnout. Rock albums constitute the backbone of both the LP and CD formats, but the aesthetic form is wearing thin. CDs have stretched the album concept out of shape. In short, CDs hold too many songs. Quantity fatally compromises quality. Simply put, seventy-four minutes and forty-two seconds are far better suited to a symphony than a collection of popular songs. Even the most accomplished pop artists can't be expected to keep up a level of rapturous engagement—in other words, genuinely hold one's interest—for more than three or four five-minute songs per hour. The album format—forty minutes divided into two discrete twenty-minute sides—was seriously undermined by the CD player and its programming function. This bells-and-whistles option makes it possible to play your favorite CD tracks in the desired sequence again and again, while blissfully ignoring the rest of the album. Perhaps a historical note is required: Vinyl LP sides were usually played without interruption because most people couldn't be bothered to keep getting up to lift the needle. The power of CD programming—enhanced selection—wields a subversive and lasting effect on pop music consumers. Apparently, the driving urge behind the dread practice of home taping wasn't satiated by the compact disc.

**chapter 9**

# CANNED MUSIC'S LAST STAND

FOR THE MUSIC BUSINESS, compact discs were a curse disguised as a blessing. The damned things were booby-trapped, like a Trojan horse. The triumph of CD over LP turned out to be a hollow victory. Consumers found out the hidden truth before record companies did—that compact discs didn't have to be playback-only. The CD code had been cracked. For the music industry, the worst nightmares of the early eighties were about to come true. Home taping is a Halloween prank compared to what you can now accomplish with a home computer and a high-speed Internet connection. By the end of the 1990s, recorded music could be lifted, liberated from its package, reproduced, and reconstituted. In current parlance, CDs can now be *ripped* (music transferred to computer files) and *burned* (music files transferred to blank discs).

Thanks to a process called peer-to-peer (P2P) file sharing, computer users copy files that are stored on each other's computers. P2P file sharing became widespread within two years, from 1999 to 2001, thanks to a software program (later a web site) called Napster. A college dropout named Shawn Fanning began writing code to help his roommates, who were collecting music on their home computers. They had just discovered MP3, a new kind of high-compression file that stowed a lot of music in a little space. Scouring the web for MP3s, Fanning's buddies became fed up with poky search engines. In January 1999, Fanning left Northeastern University to work full time on Napster. His uncle John, a local Internet entrepreneur, offered support and financial assistance. John Fanning perceived and promoted Napster as a business; Shawn pursued it for the love of technology (nineteen year olds can afford to be high-minded). By summer, Napster.com was up and running. Soon literally thousands of people were downloading the free Napster software every day. Like books in the public library, all the music on Napster.com was free.

Then came the deluge. Peer-to-peer file sharing eliminated the middleman in the recorded music market and cut out the cash register. Napster of course never made any money, but so what? Lots of grandiose Internet schemes never generated profits. Napster certainly attracted investors, as do many Internet businesses. Perhaps Napster never even tried to make money; it surely wasn't designed for that purpose.

This computerized swap meet rapidly morphed into a worldwide phenomenon. The file-trading network multiplied by the millions, at home and abroad, everyone pooling their musical booty into a huge communal treasure chest. There were 13.6 million U.S. Napster users in early 2001, when the service was running at the peak of its popularity.

Obviously, the music industry couldn't take this threat lying down. What Napster and others were doing was clearly copyright infringement. The major record companies, now controlled by entertainment conglomerates, retaliated with lawsuits. Their trade group, the RIAA, drummed up a storm of publicity. Years of

RIAA lobbying in Washington, D.C., guaranteed a congressional inquiry into the matter, complete with hearings, star testimony, and attention-grabbing headlines.

Napster wasn't the only file-sharing offender, just the most popular and visible. This made Napster an easy target, but gave it the added value of brand name recognition. Trying to create a scapegoat or offer a sacrificial lamb led to mixed results, the RIAA having succeeded in giving Napster loads of free publicity and making its own spokespeople sound like shrill demagogues. Their plan worked in the short run: Napster.com was shuttered in summer 2001 and the company finally declared bankruptcy in fall 2002. The legal song and dance had been a protracted battle, with Napster hustling to raise funds and cut deals up to the very end. Yet the fundamental problem remained, despite the public demise of Napster itself. File sharing was far from over. The P2P technology behind Napster was still out there, being refined and improved—and spreading.

A virus had invaded the music business, one that couldn't be eradicated. Clones of the Napster service immediately filled the void. The next generation of P2P thrived on sites such as KaZaA, Grokster, and Morpheus. The KaZaA Media Desktop software had 8.3 million American users in June 2002. During the week of September 15, 2002, according to download.com, KaZaA Media Desktop was downloaded 2.75 million times.

Extreme measures would be required to defeat such rampant piracy. The major labels decided it was time to fight fire with fire—but doing so also doubles the risk of being burned. Today's format conflict already resembles a guerilla war. Future battles over file sharing could end up like Vietnam if the record companies aren't careful.

In July 2002, U.S. Representative Howard Berman of Los Angeles, California, sponsored legislation that would "protect copyright holders from liability for any damage they may cause while using software to disrupt file-sharing services and search public files on consumers' computers for illegal reproductions of copyrighted music." These disruptions would be caused by technological countermeasures—echoes of cold war espionage! Copyright holders wanted to sabotage the copyright pirates, to beat them at their own game.

The Berman bill translated as a mandate for legalized home computer invasions: hacking the hackers. This tactic is tricky because it risks alienating consumers. Technological countermeasures included such preemptive moves as interdiction, spoofs, and redirection. Interdiction is the most radical means of copyright protection: an avalanche of bogus requests shuts down a file-sharing service. Spoofs are booby traps, fake files, and distorted or aborted songs disguised as coveted items. Redirection sends an unsuspecting file trader, someone duped by a decoy track, to another site where CDs are for sale.

During 2002, a more subversive tactic surfaced. Record companies have been quietly releasing protected CDs; just how many, nobody knows for sure. These "secure" CDs can't be copied, with the predictable result of further angering consumers, who are fed up with limitations on the way they consume music. At this point, not all prerecorded CDs are created equal, and this no doubt has wreaked further havoc in the record business. Simply put, record companies will not be able to regain control by sabotaging their own products. The practice is downright perverse.

Peer-to-peer file sharing does, however, have an Achilles heel: privacy is not protected, as it is in home taping. You can be peered at while you're doing anything on the Internet. In 2003, the battle over file sharing got personal. The RIAA switched the target of its lawsuits, from the P2P networks to individual file sharers. In January, Judge John D. Bates of the federal district court in Washington, D.C., ruled that the phone company Verizon had to supply the RIAA with the name of an Internet subscriber. This man stood accused of making available hundreds of illegal downloads on his home computer. In retrospect, the next step is obvious: to go after big-time MP3 pirates on college campuses. In March, four college students were sued by the RIAA. Each young man was accused of acting as a virtual download central, providing a cache of unlicensed music for his peers at Princeton, Michigan Tech, or Rensselaer Polytechnic Institute in New York; their cases were settled, each paying around $15,000. That was only the first volley. A gaggle of major Internet providers was then subpoenaed, including Comcast, Earthlink, Time Warner Cable, and Pacific Bell. Universities felt the heat as well. Total lawsuits approached 1,000 by July, with no end in sight. The word was out.

RIAA sent the following "gotcha" instant message to active KaZaA and Grokster users online during summer 2003.

COPYRIGHT INFRINGEMENT WARNING: It appears that you are offering copyrighted music to others from your computer. Distributing or downloading music on the Internet without permission from the copyright owner is ILLEGAL. It hurts songwriters who create and musicians who perform the music that you love, and all the other people who bring you music. When you break the law, you risk legal penalties. There is a simple way to avoid that risk: DON'T STEAL MUSIC either by offering it to others to copy or downloading it on a "file-sharing system" like this.

Right or wrong, record companies can be seen as self-defeating zealots who treat consumers—that is, potential customers—as criminals. This isn't very likely to stimulate CD sales.

## Back in the Day

> As Napster grew and ultimately hit its peak, if you look at CD sales [they] were up as long as Napster was popular. The point at which Napster started filtering (blocking out certain songs after a court order in March 2001) is the point at which the record industry announced that the constant increase in their CD sales suddenly changed.
>
> —Shawn Fanning, *Wall Street Journal*, October 2002

Before the emergence of Napster and file sharing, a few artists valiantly struggled with selling their music on the Internet. They didn't find it any easier than did the record companies. At the time, the Net offered unlimited—and undefined—sales potential. A few vanguard acts viewed it as a tantalizing escape route from record-company dependency, but this escape route led into a torturous maze. You can give away music on the Net, but selling it has always been a different story.

In 1999, the rapper Chuck D (Carleton Ridenhour) of Public Enemy told it like it was. He already had a reputation for being articulate, radical, and prone to shooting straight from the hip, and his take on the burgeoning Internet was typically scathing. "The execs, lawyers and accountants who lately have made most of the money in the music biz are now running scared from the technology that evens out the creative field and makes artists harder to pimp."

Hip-hop DJs always existed at the cutting edge of music technology. So it comes as no surprise that two groundbreaking rap groups of the late eighties plunged into the Internet music scene ten years later. Testing the waters while others watched, Public Enemy and the Beastie Boys each took the plunge in summer 1998. Both groups posted free digital recordings on their web sites. They were giving away their music.

Net-savvy Beastie Boys fans could download a selection of live tracks accompanying the recently released *Hello Nasty* album. (Canny marketers at heart, the Beastie Boys methodically generated a valuable e-mail list of 100,000 digital dabblers.) Inevitably, the punky white rappers had their knuckles rapped by their label, Capitol, in fall 1998, and they caved in to the pressure. By December, Capitol persuaded the thirty-something Boys to drop the digital giveaway, pronto. By April 1999, the hip-hop trio was offering remixed tracks and video clips on their official site with the record company's full approval. Not long afterward, the Beastie Boys renewed their contract with Capitol Records. Their multiyear deal was estimated to be worth around $30 million.

Between its politics and polemics, Public Enemy wasn't as cagey or lucky as were the Beastie Boys. Chuck D and company broke with their long-standing label, Def Jam, a record company that never tried to censor or even influence the group's controversial lyrics and complex music. So this particular split was a serious sign of dissension. Public Enemy bounced to an Internet start-up label, Atomic Pop, a move that was adventurous, although doomed: typically, the label proved short-lived. A digital version of *There's a Poison Going On*, the group's subsequent release, was made available online for two months before the CD showed up in retail stores. Unfortunately, Public Enemy's sales base continued its slump, even in the new medium. Chuck D proselytized effectively, but the truth of the digital situation wasn't yet so clear. At this point, the whole phenomenon of Internet music still hung on the CD, the packaged product of record companies. That was about to change. In the meantime, Public Enemy tried to make the Net function as an alternative to record companies, as a kind of independent online label. It didn't really work, but it was a step in the right direction. Underneath his rhetorical flourishes, Chuck D must've sensed a simple truth. Technology was about to change the rules of the music business, leveling the playing field once and for all.

## Opening Salvo

In the San Diego area, a computer consultant named Michael Robertson ran a search engine clearinghouse out of his living room. He stumbled onto a nascent revolution in 1996, completely unexpectedly. Robertson noticed a mysterious request popping up on the engines again and again: MP3.

The MP3 format caused the first major battle in the Internet music wars. MP3 files represented a giant step forward for Internet music delivery. Think of it as an especially concise way of encoding music in digital zeros and ones: supercompact storage coupled with easy retrieval. Before the MP3, WAV and MIDI files comprised the first delivery formats for Internet music. In the early nineties, they were about the only game in town. One grave drawback was built into WAVs and MIDIs—it took hours to download mere minutes of music. WAV is a Microsoft format for use on Windows only. Since these files aren't compressed, like MP3 files, WAV delivers high-quality sound—and download at a turtle's pace. MIDI (Musical Instrument Digital Interface) files were mostly used to store data on electronic keyboards and synthesizers, though they could also be transferred to computer and played back.

MP3 is shorthand for MPEG–1 Layer Three. MPEG is an acronym for Motion Picture Experts Group. This committee of engineers is part of the International Organization for Standardization in Geneva. In 1992, they established the MPEG formula. Initially, MPEG was used to compress digital video into small computer files. After a while, word circulated that MPEG could also reduce digital audio, without losing the sound quality of a CD. MPEG–1 Layer Three was capable of fitting songs into files twelve times smaller than the preceding WAV files. A five-minute song once hogged fifty megabytes; now it could be comfortably stored in five megabytes. Download time nearly disappeared, or so it seemed. The new format translated hours of waiting back into minutes. Supercompression also increased the volume of a disc. Using MP3, a single CD-ROM could accommodate a full dozen albums of music.

College students converted to the new format with missionary zeal. They're the perfect demographic to spread the gospel: music obsessed and technologically savvy. Many college students gained frequent access to speedy Net service via their large school computer systems—and college students by definition have too much time on their hands.

In 1995, Progressive Audio introduced its Real Audio software. Marketed as the Real Player, it captured the public imagination—

and a spot in the marketplace—before MP3 could really spread its tentacles. Real Audio players made it possible to listen to musical bits while you downloaded a song; the process of listening to music this way, "live" on the web, became known as *streaming*. In April 1996, the web site DJ.com launched the concept of Internet radio. Using Real Audio streams, the early DJ.com offered twenty-four channels of music.

During the next couple of years, high-speed Internet connections became commonplace. The method of music consumption shifted from streaming (hear now) to downloading (save for later). After downloading MP3 files into your computer, you needed a software program to play them. Developed by Nullsoft, the popular Winamp player performed the same function as the old-fashioned hardware (that is, the phonograph), only now the record player is inside the computer—and no records.

In 1998, Robertson founded the web site MP3.com. and presented it as a clearinghouse for new music, a repository of songs stored in the new format. At the very start, the web site focused on unknown artists, who could agree freely to post their music online, unlike musicians signed to a major record label. Moreover, those downloaded files came scot-free; MP3.com generated much of its income from advertising. By 1998, the young web site claimed 150,000 visitors a day. By spring 2001, MP3.com attracted nearly one million regular users overall.

For fiscal 2000, MP3.com's revenues hit $80 million, a 266 percent improvement over the previous year. At the same time, MP3.com posted a $23 million loss. For an Internet start-up, it easily could've been worse. By then, however, MP3 also stood for something else in many people's minds: copyright infringement.

Blame it on the burners. More and more, personal computers came equipped with a CD-RW drive known as a *CD burner* (RW stands for rewriteable). Unlike CD-ROM, music or text could be recorded on CD-RW discs. Sales of blank CD-RW discs soared.

Prerecorded music CDs could be converted—ripped—into computerized MP3 files; and MP3 files could be reconverted—burned—back onto a standard disc. Of course, the capacity of that homemade CD returned to the traditional seventy-four minutes. The software circle was now complete—with record companies effectively removed from the loop. Predictably, this unfettered technology and accompanying freedom-of-information rhetoric did not sit well with the increasingly nervous music industry.

In the first month of the new century, MP3.com welcomed a bold sibling. Somewhat naively, Robertson thought he'd finessed the copyright complications and record company concerns. On MyMP3.com, users could listen to their CD collection online. The musical contents were tucked away in "virtual lockers." Once your purchased copy of a prerecorded disc was scanned (to prove ownership), you gained access to a copy stored online. From that point on, it's yours to rip and burn.

Access could be gained from any Internet connection, anytime, anywhere. MyMP3.com users could program their own albums and select their own playlists, an attractive proposition. MP3.com owned and controlled all the name-brand material—a.k.a. copyrighted recordings—on the web site, and the music files were stored on its computers, so users gain access only to the songs already owned, guaranteed. All the bases were covered. What's not to like?

The industry responded with lawsuits, instantly. Record companies didn't appreciate that proof-of-ownership ploy. Neither did music publishers.

That spring, a copyright violation came before Judge Jed S. Rakoff of the federal district court in Manhattan. He ruled against MyMP3.com, determining that its database of 80,000 CDs was being used in violation of copyright law. So the web site was shuttered in April, scarcely three months old.

In a later ruling, the same judge directed MP3.com to fork over a hefty royalty settlement to Universal Music Group, $25,000 per CD used on the web site, an extraordinary sum. An undisclosed settlement was reached out of court for much less, but the point was clear. This was war: take no prisoners. Eventually, MP3.com settled the virtual locker dispute with the five titans in the record cartel: BMG, EMI, Sony, Warner, and Universal. The music publishers—ASCAP and BMI—also received their piece of the pie.

The copyright suit squelched MyMP3.com for seven long months in 2000. As a fall from grace, it was truly humbling. MyMP3.com finally resurfaced as a sort of shadow, a weak reflection of its former glory. With no major-label talent in the locker, the resurrected MyMP3.com remained a bush-league music service.

The online music locker controversy was eventually settled to the tune of $130 million, paid by MP3.com to the record companies. Adding irony to injury, MP3.com was bought by Vivendi in May 2001; the French telecommunications giant paid $372 million. And yet another Net music movement stole the media thunder from MP3.com during 2000 and 2001. A new software program took the concept of downloading music and turned it into a virtual free-for-all. The MP3 mess is child's play compared with what came next: the Napster melodrama.

## Napster Holds No Patents

In 1999, ex-freshman Shawn Fanning set out to build the proverbial better mousetrap and named his invention Napster, in honor of a childhood nickname. Setting out to refine a search engine, he specifically designed a program that could reel in MP3 files *quickly*. Napster enabled Net users to share—and copy—MP3 files with a minimum of fuss and muss.

On a standard web site, users receive information from a central source, or server. In a peer-to-peer network, users receive and send information. Each participating computer becomes a source or server. Downloading the Napster software empowered users: you could now transfer, index, and catalogue music files at will. Napster itself was not a new format; rather, it rendered an existing format—MP3—more accessible. For Net regulars, MP3 files suddenly became easy to track down. Type in a song title and artist's name and see the list of users who have that tune on file. Select a source and download. The MP3 file copies from one hard drive to another. Napster was not so much an under-the-counter retailer as it was an enormous and illicit library.

Some Napster enthusiasts insist it wasn't just about the download. Using Napster enrolled you in a community, they suggest. Not only songs were shared, but broader musical tastes and habits, the most personal of information. Musical passions were communicated and expanded via the technologically enhanced transfer of computer files.

In January 1999, Napster started handing out free downloads of its software. A few months later, Napster, Inc. was formed in San Mateo, California. Plans existed to commercialize the product, but downloads of the software program itself were always offered free of charge. Revenue—admittedly not a major concern during the Internet boom—would come from advertising.

Shawn teamed up with his uncle, John Fanning, who previously owned Netgames, an online gaming site. John held as much as 70 percent of Napster initially, having supplied much of the capital. Shawn supplied a winning, low-key charm as the company's public face. At nineteen, he made a shuffling, brilliant, anti-icon, a man of baseball caps and a few carefully chosen words. His share of the company never exceeded 3 percent to 5 percent. His uncle considered that stake to be a better-than-average deal for somebody in his position—that is, the inventor.

Elaine Richardson, a venture capitalist from Boston, was hired as Napster's first chief executive officer in 1999. Surprisingly, a compromise between Napster and record companies was broached in the fall of that year. Later, *Business Week* reported that Richardson's abrasive style chafed the head honchos of the music industry. Perhaps, but whatever happened, the conversation ended there, and Napster didn't attract many glances from investment firms or corporate suitors. In fall 1999, with a sigh of relief, Napster finally received $2 million in venture capital from an outside source. The gambler was a Silicon Valley–based firm called Hummer-Winblad. By May 2000, Hummer-Winblad dropped another $15 million into Napster's till. The first order of business was unplugging Richardson and installing a new CEO. A Hummer-Winblad partner and corporate lawyer named Hank Barry was duly appointed to the hot seat.

By year's end, Napster passed the million-download mark. At that point, the record companies—through the RIAA—filed a copyright infringement suit, in December 1999. Through the early months of the new century, scores of colleges and universities banned Napster. From New York University and Cal Berkeley to Indiana and Notre Dame, the massive school computer systems were log-jammed by students downloading music from the controversial site.

## Noble Opposition

In April 2000, the hard rock band Metallica sued Napster for copyright infringement. One month later, Napster cut loose more than 300,000 users for the heinous crime of downloading Metallica songs. Two weeks after Metallica, the hardcore rapper and hip-hop producer Dr. Dre filed his own suit against Napster. There's a delicate irony contained in Dre's stance. Part of the good doctor's mad genius rests in his canny ability to duplicate classic breaks and beats on synthesizer keyboards, rather than sample old records and pay the accompanying licensing fees. In general, Napster was opposed by superstar-level performers and embraced by struggling up-and-comers. That divisive class warfare was unpleasant, but also perfectly understandable.

At that point, Napster was being used by nearly one million people per day.

Napster insisted it wasn't liable because it didn't keep any music on its computers. Napster's lawyers employed the "fair use" defense, arguing that the same legal rights that protect home taping of video and music must cover copying a CD for personal use.

The Betamax decision was most often cited as precedent for Napster's defense. When the movie industry tried to squelch the VCR in the early 1980s, the U.S. Supreme Court ultimately ruled in favor of Sony, in 1984. The Court acknowledged that VCRs could be used for a legitimate purpose—that is, home taping for individual use. On one hand, it can't be denied that Napster made it possible to copy CDs at a far greater magnitude than would have been possible otherwise. On the other hand, consider the history of video: Hollywood film studios eventually made pots of money on prerecorded cassettes, despite widespread home taping.

On June 13, 2000, the battle royal began. The RIAA filed a motion for preliminary injunction to block all major-label content shared or traded on Napster. Apparently, Napster saw the threat coming and continued to stand firm, confident of beating the charge. John Fanning claimed to be a diligent student of copyright law as it applied to digital music, and that he was specifically acquainted with the decisions of the Ninth Circuit Court of Appeals. So the Napster forces entered the legal fray utterly convinced that their brand of peer-to-peer file sharing would prevail in the U.S. court system.

Heavy-hitting support was quickly arranged, however, just in case. A few days after the RIAA motion, Hank Barry brought in the legal superstar David Boies. At this time, mid June 2000, Boies was widely hailed as the lawyer who had triumphed over Microsoft in the Justice Department's antitrust case. He was not yet known as the lawyer who failed to salvage the contested Florida election for presidential candidate Al Gore.

On July 26, U.S. District Judge Marilyn Patel ruled in favor of the record industry. Judge Patel ordered Napster to halt major-label content trade in (little more than) forty-eight hours. Two days later, just nine hours before shutdown, the Ninth U.S. Circuit Court of Appeals ruled that the company should be allowed to continue operating.

Napster made its appeal in October 2000. The decision came down four months later and it was unanimous—against Napster. The three-judge panel at the Ninth Circuit Court of Appeals backed Judge Patel's earlier decision. Napster was also declared liable for user's copyright infringement. In other words, they had to pay the equivalent of royalties on music that had already been downloaded. The judges' decision on the appeal stressed that peer-to-peer services are not inherently illegal, just the Napster application itself—a point that foreshadowed the immediate future.

At this point there were twenty-one million registered Napster users. On any given night, 500,000 of them signed on—which gave Napster one-third the number of AOL's audience in the same time slot.

## Net of Thieves

The Court of Appeals found that the injunction is not only warranted, but required. And it ruled in our favor on every legal issue presented.

—Hilary Rosen, Recording Industry
Association of America, 2000

The major labels were asleep at the switch. They are asleep no longer.

—Richard Parsons, president,
AOL Time Warner, Inc., 2000

They [Napster users] can't all be criminals.
—Thomas Middlehoff, CEO, Bertelsmann AG, 2000

At the darkest hour, support came from an unlikely quarter. In November, Napster announced an alliance with Bertelsmann, its first successful attempt to deal with the record companies. The proposal centered on a subscription fee charged by Napster, with part of the fee distributed as royalty payments to record companies. More savage irony: this arrangement will be financed, in part, by one of the very companies who fought to close down the rogue file-sharing network. The German-based entertainment conglomerate eventually coughed up $85 million for the Napster deal.

Bertelsmann CEO Thomas Middlehoff and Napster founder Shawn Fanning performed an odd-couple act for the media. Their joint venture was announced at a plush press conference in New York City. The dapper middle-aged executive and the young man in a University of Michigan cap consummated their deal, clutching shoulders in a celebratory bear hug. Slightly more than fifty years previous, the long-playing record debuted in much the same fashion. One crucial distinction is that LP inventor Peter Goldmark was a CBS employee (if not always a "company man"). At the turn of the twenty-first century, the music industry no longer controlled the technology on which it depended. Now record companies were compelled to court inventors and technological upstarts or else seek to impede them in the courts à la James Petrillo of the AFM. Bertelsmann tried to attract other record companies to the Napster cause, but there were no takers. The grand experiment never got off the ground. By this point, the count on Napster users was thirty-eight million and rising.

Suddenly, the jig was up. The deadline passed in spring 2001. Napster had to pull down its copyrighted major-label tracks or shut down the service completely. Metallica and Dr. Dre songs were promptly removed from Napster, but copying persisted on the sly. Song titles were purposely misspelled by the users, coded in slang to foil the filters. As it turns out, the "protected files" weren't all that secure.

Napster shut down for a spell in the summer then reemerged, vanquished. Cleansed of major-label content, the revived service—call it Napster II—looked like a burned-out shell of its former self. Napster use plummeted, along with the departure of all that pirated brand-name music. In a month's time, half as many users were logging on, a catastrophic loss. Other peer-to-peer services emerged to answer the demand. Skirting around the law was a breeze.

## Gnutella and Others

What we want is someone to think twice before they start a business.

—Hilary Rosen, Recording Industry
Association of America, 2001

Gnutella was not a web site, a company, or a product. It was a protocol: a set of rules that guided peer-to-peer computer file sharing. Gnutella connected users' computers without relying on a central computer, as did Napster. Thus it was harder to stop. Free downloadable software for Gnutella was readily available on the Internet. Introduced in March 2000, Gnutella allowed users to exchange music and other files. When the Napster battles raged, searches for Gnutella software spread like wildfire.

Justin Frankel and Tom Pepper devised the original program for Gnutella. Heads of a programming team at AOL Time Warner's Music Division, they'd already become Net millionaires. They sold their start-up company (Nullsoft) to AOL. At Nullsoft, they'd launched the popular Winamp MP3 player. At their new AOL gig, Frankel and Pepper started work on an alternative file-sharing program. Their major motivation stemmed from a belief that Napster was headed toward oblivion. They didn't want to see the peer-to-peer concept disappear with it. When the bosses got wind of what was going on in the software lab, AOL Time Warner put its foot down—too late.

The Gnutella protocol was now the property of a program-mers network, circulating among hundreds of collaborators who helped to refine the software program and spread it around even further. (In a sense, this setup resembles the free Linux op-erating system.) The file-sharing genie was out of the bottle. Since Gnutella allows users to trade video, text, and graphics as well as audio, now pornography and pirated computer pro-grams coexisted with the music. Neither the movie industry nor the music business was happy about that. A generation of tech-savvy consumers who completely ignored copyright law was truly something to worry about. The CD was their parents' recording format.

KaZaA, a popular file-sharing program developed by an Amsterdam-based company called Fast Track, operated differ-ently from Gnutella and Napster. Instead of a central directory, KaZaA created *supernodes*, or search hubs, along the network. Individual computers formed a chain of minidirectories among active users. "Consumers are making a statement that $18 is not the right price for a CD," declared Niklas Zenstrom, president of Fast Track, in 2001. "But the record companies aren't giving them an alternative."

Aimster was another free-download software program for peer-to-peer file sharing. Aimster utilized AOL's popular instant message and buddy lists features. (E-mail stays on your computer until you read it; instant messages disappear when the on-screen interface concludes.) Aimster allowed users to swap files via the instant message system. The so-called buddy lists kept Aimster users informed about who else is on-line and in the trading mode. Justin Frankel developed an early software program for this instant-message file sharing called AIMazing, and his bosses at AOL liked it even less than Gnutella.

More than two million people regularly used Aimster by February 2001. Three months later, predictably, the RIAA initiated a lawsuit against Aimster for copyright infringement. In his defense, the developer of Aimster, Johnny Deep, sincerely contended that Aimster was intended as an instant message system. The previous winter, though, he had crowed to the *New York Post*, "if Napster were to swallow the poison pill, we could take off." More or less, that is exactly what happened.

## Napster Wraps

Naturally, the major record labels viewed Napster as a gang of rank opportunists, amateurs launching a business without a business plan. For a while, Bertelsmann had money to burn on Middlehoff's consuming interest in Net music, since it was the only media conglomerate not financially tied to the film business. In addition, the prospect of further deals with record companies offered a neat solution to Napster's vaguely addressed problem: How do you take a hugely popular Net service and actually make it profitable? The example recently set by Microsoft's *Slate* magazine and ESPN's SportsZone had been troubling, to say the least. These two successful web sites switched to pay-to-play then watched visitor traffic start to disappear. Subscription fees had to be jettisoned in both cases.

Meanwhile, the clock ticked on Napster. Negotiations with Bertelsmann dragged and stalled well into 2002. The summer ouster of CEO Thomas Middlehoff, Napster's great champion at Bertelsmann, surely didn't help settle matters. A settlement was pursued even after Middlehoff was out of the picture. Bertelsmann offered to pay off Napster's debts and buy its assets, but they couldn't agree on terms. There were many reports of disarray at Napster; John Fanning eventually filed suit against the other members of the board. Finally, Shawn Fanning and other Napster top executives resigned in May 2002. Napster declared bankruptcy one month later. By then, negotiations with Bertelsmann had collapsed and Napster was broke. Bertelsmann still wanted to buy the remaining assets, possibly to use the name for a new service, but a Delaware bankruptcy court forbade Bertelsmann's acquisition in September 2002. Liquidation, rather than reorganization, was the inevitable next step.

Napster had been off-line since July 2001, but its effect is still being felt. Asked about the effect of file sharing on CD sales, Shawn Fanning still defended the practice in late 2002. "It may be hurting the music industry at this point," he admitted. "But my view is the consumers have the ability to learn about new and interesting music, and the barrier is lowered in a way that gives them control over how they experience it. I think those are positive things."

It's safe to say that the MP3 format was never intended to be the exclusive preserve of bootleggers and pirates. The point was to achieve a quick and easy transfer of music, from CD to personal computers and portable players. Consumer demand remains high, the technology is more than ready, but the record companies lag behind the technological pace. The seductive allure of the MP3 format is all about selection and portability, not thievery and deceit.

The Napster crisis offered a window of opportunity. Some clever soul in the music business might deduce a way to charge a nominal fee per song: miniscule amounts, perhaps, but those nickels and dimes add up. Until then, the idea of leveling web site subscription fees will be met with stiff resistance. The free stuff is much easier to obtain, and so far there's been much more of it. All along, the almighty power of selection has been driving the runaway popularity of Napster and its spawn, such as KaZaA and Morpheus.

Digital music offers enhanced choice, while it also jacks up the consumer's level of convenience and flexibility. Napster was not blameless in this affair: musicians deserve fair compensation for their labors. But the success of Napster identified a fresh appetite in the music-buying public. The record companies ignore these hungry cries at their peril. Instead of feeding dissatisfied customers, they've tried to discredit any competing technology. This strategy of resistance didn't work for James Petrillo and the AFM in their fight against canned music. The truce after the Napster fight was temporary, truculent, and illusory. This promises to be a fight to the finish.

## Hardware as Software

The portable MP3 player was the hardware component of the sound-compression technology. In October 1998, Diamond Multimedia Systems, Inc., introduced its RIO PMP 300. Though it stored just sixty minutes of music, the RIO player boasted a reasonable price, retailing for less than $200. This handheld MP3 player engaged the roaming ears of a restless listening public. With any purchase of a player, Diamond supplied a free software program for converting CDs into MP3 files.

The music industry didn't much cotton to that technological innovation either. The RIAA applied for a court order preventing sales of the Diamond RIO player. The judge denied their request, and the so-called killer app proliferated. Electronics manufacturers fell over each other in the rush to produce digital audio products that would work in tandem with personal computers.

The Nomad Jukebox, courtesy of the Singapore-based outfit Creative Technology, represented the next step in portable digital. Nomad debuted in late 2000. Though it fit the size and shape of a standard CD player, the Nomad lived up to its name: featuring a whopping 100 hours of storage time (roughly 1,500 songs), the Nomad really was a *mobile* jukebox.

The ultimate app, at least for now, may well be iPOD. Introduced by MacIntosh in late 2001, the iPOD attracted media attention with its sleek design and capacious storage. Weighing 6.5 ounces, the iPOD fits in your pocket, the size of a cigarette pack. Its 5-gigbyte hard drive holds 66 hours of music; that's roughly 1,300 songs or 130 albums. A high-resolution screen displays song title, artist, and album (if the MP3 files contain that information). This was portability perfected, at least until Creative Technology unveiled the Nomad Muvo. The size of a cigarette lighter (or fat stick of gum), the Muvo contains 64 megabytes of music, or 15 to 20 songs. The player's bottom half is a solid-state memory unit that slips off and plugs the Muvo into the USB connector on the back of your personal computer for easy downloading. The Nomad Muvo resembles a sort of reprogrammable hardware, a postsoftware music player. Behold the portable album.

For the remaining turntable fanciers who aren't DJs, rarefied machines are available. These turntables redefine a fabled 1950s concept: stratospherically high-end hi-fi for the new century. The Rockport System III Sirius suggests a high-tech rendition of an antique. Hand tooled by an engineer over a period of six months, this Ferrarilike turntable weighs 550 pounds and costs $73,750. There were twenty-five or so of them in existence in 2001. The Sirius suspends the record and tone arm on a cushion of compressed air. A magnetic-induction motor keeps the disc spinning without touching the turntable mat, so the sole physical contact occurs between needle and record. If you have to ask how great it actually sounds, then you definitely can't afford it.

## Software Is Nowhere

> If it becomes a format war, it will ruin the whole thing.
> —Stan Goman, Chief Operating Officer,
> Tower Records, 1999

Software was the last frontier in the digital music wars. In the late 1990s, two spanking-new silver discs were hyped as the future of recorded music—and guess what? Backed by two different music-biz consortiums, these variations on the disc happened to be completely incompatible with each other. Given the historical record, how could that be?

This latest software struggle begins in 1997. Compact disc sales were stagnant and mainstream musical taste had turned stale, shifting from rock and country to pop and hip-hop. The time had come for a technological nudge, a format change.

The Digital Video Disc format, or DVD, debuted around this time. Commercial acceptance was enthusiastic and almost instantaneous. To the film industry's delight, the DVD was playback-only. Given the rapid sales of the new video players and discs, DVD Audio appeared a logical progression and to some, a solid bet in a suddenly volatile marketplace. A forum of ten companies united behind the new format: electronics giants such as Hitachi and Toshiba held hands with content providers like AOL Time Warner and Universal.

DVD Audio contained seventy-four minutes of sound, just like a standard CD. The bulked-up sound quality came (at least in part) from DVD Audio's six channels of sound, like quadrophonic with two more added on. Incredibly, that means purchasing a new player with six speakers. "Six-channel surround sound" may well appeal to the growing number of people who harbor a DVD "home theater" setup in their den or basement. The only drawback was a familiar, nagging complaint: DVD Audio discs didn't play on traditional DVD machines. Purchasing a new DVD Audio player was unavoidable.

The scheme behind DVD Audio is a familiar ruse: the industry expected that sheeplike consumers would replace their musty CD albums with this state-of-the-art software. Can lightning really strike twice? After the sudden death of vinyl, perhaps consumers were wary, afraid of being burned again.

DVD Audio's opponent in this old-fashioned format war—battle of the speeds revisited—went by a rather military-sounding acronym, SACD, for Super Audio CD. Backed by Sony and Phillips, SACD was directed away from the mainstream and instead targeted the audiophile market.

Sony unveiled SACD at a 1999 press conference. Nobuyuki Idei, the company's president, touted the new format as the sonic equivalent of analog. Here was an unlikely, brilliant instance of closure: What goes around comes around. "When we introduced CD in 1981," recalled Idei, "most people were satisfied with the great sound—especially for pop and rock. Yet some people prefer analog. Audio purists remain loyal to analog."

Super Audio CD contained slightly more music—110 minutes—than the rival format. Unlike the DVD Audio players, Super Audio CD players accommodated a traditional compact disc, and many SACDs could be played in a standard CD player. Confused? So were most music consumers. Neither DVD Audio nor SACD was exactly a commercial juggernaut. The initial number of titles released in both configurations is miniscule, barely topping 100 discs in either SACD or DVD Audio—a paucity that reflects a considerable lack of interest in new recorded music software, or at least in recorded music software that must be purchased. The right kind of recording, however, may yet provide ignition for the new format: perhaps something to demonstrate its enhanced audio quality, something along the lines of sound effects or exotic percussion.

DataPlay may be a final, desperate ploy for physical music software. DataPlay discs are 1-inch-wide discs holding a little less music than a CD-ROM, but with comparable sound quality.

Once again, the new discs (software) dictate the purchase of a new player (hardware). The latter function as portable music players, or as drives plugged into a personal computer. But the DataPlay discs are copy protected. That means the files—the music—can't be ripped into a computer or burned onto a CD. At first, the tiny discs were intended as a storage format for digital cameras. Steve Volk, who founded the Colorado-based DataPlay, Inc. in 1998, eventually flashed on the musical potential of his new minidiscs. He also recognized their utility for "protecting" or controlling content. Concerned with piracy, eager for a secure new format, the record companies signed on with DataPlay. A flood of prerecorded disc releases from the major labels was expected to launch the format. At the same time, though, a nasty rumor kept circulating: the music software of the future would be no software at all.

### Too Little Too Late?

Even with Napster in ruins, peer-to-peer file trading ran rampant on the Net. Alternate sharing services flourished. The cat remained out of the bag, despite threats and impending lawsuits from the RIAA. It took a while, thanks to the royalty demands of songwriters and music publishers, but in late 2001, the record companies finally unveiled their digital music platforms. After years of foot-dragging, this ballyhooed pair of on-line debuts arrived as a distinct anticlimax, if not a flat-out disaster.

Musicnet was a joint venture between EMI, Bertelsmann, AOL Time Warner, and Real Networks. Users paid approximately $10 per month for the right to stream and download a designated number of songs, around 100. The fee allowed customers to listen to their selections for a month, so in effect, you were renting the music rather than owning it. Keep listening past the thirty-day deadline, and another charge would appear on next month's statement.

Press Play teamed Universal and Sony with Yahoo! and the Microsoft Network. For $10 and change, Press Play allows users to download and stream a selection of songs. One slight but significant improvement over Musicnet was offered: On Press Play, downloaded songs can be replayed indefinitely, as long as you pay your subscription fee. One major drawback, though, is that the music from both sites *gets stuck inside your computer.* Songs from Press Play and Musicnet can't be converted to CD or transferred to portable MP3 players. While both sites draw on song libraries of 100,000 titles or more, neither cover the catalogues of all five major record companies. And the best-selling artists who control their own web rights aren't included. Legitimate downloads of the Beatles, the Eagles, or Led Zeppelin are not to be found.

Rhapsody, launched by Listen.com with music supplied by the major labels, represents a small step forward. For its monthly fee of $10, Rhapsody offers subscribers an extra degree of freedom. That's the initial draw: unlimited streaming and some burning, at 99¢ a song, but no MP3 downloading. In its first year, Rhapsody amassed a larger song library than any of the other legal services; yet there are still major gaps in content.

At this point, the music business needed a white knight. Enter Steve Jobs, the chief executive of Apple Computer, on horseback. Apple's online iTunes Music Store opened for business on April 28, 2003. "Consumers don't want to be treated like criminals and artists don't want their valuable work stolen," declared Jobs at the San Francisco launch. "The iTunes Music Store offers a groundbreaking solution for both." The story of iTunes will be a case study, a test run. Leaving the corporate war on piracy aside for a moment, can a pay-as-you-play downloading service survive on the Internet—that is, pay off for the music industry *and* satisfy customers?

The iTunes pitch is simple: No subscription fee, 99¢ downloads. iTunes users are granted more freedom than any other pay service subscribers. For their 99¢, iTunes customers can download a song onto an unlimited number of iPod players as well as three Apple MacIntosh computers. They can also burn up to ten CDs with the same playlist. The initial iTunes library included 200,000 songs. (A thirty-second sample or preview is available for many songs.)

Employing charisma and, perhaps, connections, Jobs convinced No Doubt and the Eagles to license their music online for the first time. The iTunes Music Store drew the bulk of its merchandise from the five usual suspects: Warner, BMG, EMI, Sony Music, and Universal. Any deal, however, between Apple and the big music companies must have required an extra round of diplomacy. Famous for its striking ads, Apple originally marketed the iPOD (and an early version of iTunes) with the provocative slogan "Rip. Mix. Burn." Yet the music business apparently is willing to forgive and forget Apple's slap in its face, since record companies rushed to stock the shelves of the online store. Hilary Rosen, speaking in one of her last official acts before steeping down as RIAA spokesperson, delivered a ringing endorsement of the new service. The iTunes ad logo was a neck-up shot of a Gibson electric guitar—an iconic and reassuring image in place of the anarchic earlier slogan.

The response was instantaneous and electrifying. Apple reported a total of one million iTunes downloads in the first week of May 2003. That number fell to 500,000 by June. Still, half a million seems more than respectable; in fact, it seems remarkable, considering that Apple has only a 2.4 percent share of the computer market. A decade earlier, 9.4 percent of home computers were Macs. One can assume that a majority of Mac users are music fans. The introduction of iTunes shrewdly tied into the continuing success of the iPOD player; and the subsequent success of iTunes may serve another vital function for Apple: It would be a great way to boost the company's shrinking presence in the computer market. If nothing else, iTunes is off to a surprising start. The legal competition certainly noticed. Rhapsody responded by slashing its burn rate to 79¢ a song. Musicnet and Press Play had to rethink their strict burn policies. Openly targeting iTunes, AOL designed its own online music download service.

But will the illegal competition take heed? On April 25, 2003, a lower federal court in California ruled that two free song-sharing services—Grokster and Morpheus—couldn't be held liable for any copyright infringement committed by their users. U.S. District Court Judge Stephen Wilson stunned the music industry with his decision. The pirates, at least some of them, are here to stay.

Before the dust cleared, the Napster struggle already looked like a turning point for the record business. Most probably, the fight over Napster will be remembered as a lost opportunity that was tragically misapprehended as a triumph for the status quo.

All this technological change is just beginning to affect the aesthetic of pop music. For the past fifty years, music has come prepackaged in collections of ten or fifteen or so songs. From the

LP era through the CD regime, the album ruled as a creative format. The rise of digital music threw the individual song back into high relief. While the single isn't likely to return as a physical object, pop musicians are now free to concentrate on songs again. Someday soon, digital technology will inspire a new musical movement, a revolution nurtured and spread on the Internet. The catalyst will be a high-impact recording: a dramatic song or performance that defines a new style and demonstrates its range. It will be a digital-era echo of preceding twentieth-century milestones such as "O Sole Mio," "Alexander's Ragtime Band," "Crazy Blues," "The Prisoner's Song," "Pistol Packin' Mama," "How High the Moon," *Sgt.Pepper's Lonely Hearts Club Band*, *Dark Side of the Moon*, "Love to Love You, Baby," "The Adventures of Grandmaster Flash on the Wheels of Steel," and "Planet Rock."

In the year 2000, a vaguely ominous prediction appeared in *Billboard*: "Physical Sales of Music Will Top off by 2004." Don't look for those rotating discs to *completely* disappear anytime soon, however; the CD package may resemble damaged goods at this point, but its contents haven't settled or shifted. Music itself is still miraculous. It's just that the science of recording isn't as remote, mysterious, and awe-inspiring as it once was. Thanks to technology, the magic finally escaped from the can.

# AFTERMATH

"I think the downloading problem won't be solved until we're able to electronically interfere with the process. There are some new technologies being tested and I think they'll be ready pretty soon . . . very soon. In one or two years, we'll have taken care of the problem."

—Gunter Thielen, Chief Executive
of Bertelsmann AG, September 2004

THE NAPSTER BATTLE was only the beginning of a bitterly contested campaign, a fight to the finish between Big Music and millions of Internet users. If the record industry is also trying to influence the hearts and minds of digital copyright violators, then so far it has utterly failed. In September 2003, the Boston-based Yankee Group research firm estimated that 57 million Americans were sharing music files online. Ever since, the music industry has resorted to desperate measures in its fight against illegal downloading. Bluntly put, the fight got personal. By September 2004, more than 5,000 individuals had been sued by the music companies' trade group, the Recording Institute Association of America (RIAA). In many cases, the plaintiff was an unwitting computer owner being sued for his teenager's music collection. Out of the first couple of hundred culprits sued, inevitably, a poster child emerged. But Brianna La Hara couldn't have been the kind of freeloader the RIAA lawyers had in mind when they set out to make an example of somebody. Twelve-year-old Brianna was literally a poster *child*. She was also an honor student at a parochial school in New York City, and a resident of public housing. "I got really scared, my stomach is all turning," she told the *New York Post* when the suit was filed. "Out of all the people, why did they pick me?"

She couldn't have been the only person asking that question. Sylvia Torres, Brianna's mother, had mistakenly assumed KaZaA was a legal service. After all, she paid a monthly service charge. Eventually Ms. Torres settled out of court with the RIAA, for $2,000. Frankly, it was a public relations disaster for the record industry group. But one year down the road, the lawsuits keep right on coming, filed every few months in waves of several hundred at a time. So far more than 600 of these suits have been settled out of court, for amounts ranging up to $15,000.

"I've never had a situation like this before, where there are powerful plaintiffs and powerful lawyers on one side then a whole slew of ordinary folks on the other," said U.S. District Judge Nancy Gertner. According to the *Los Angeles Times*, dozens of RIAA lawsuits have passed through Judge Gertner's Boston courtroom. In a recent letter to the *New York Times*, the chairman of the RIAA defended the legal assault on file sharing. "The best approach is innovation and enforcement," wrote Mitch Bainwol on April 24, 2004. "And that's exactly what the music community is doing."

Well, the threat to the music industry *is* real. The so-called digital pirates have persisted and even prospered in the face of prosecution. In September 2004, the Big Champagne research firm estimated that 24 million Americans were using file-sharing online services like KaZaA and Grokster, mostly to trade copyrighted content like music and movies. And apart from those well-known commercial sites, file sharing has burrowed deeper underground. Many more users have formed smaller, hard-to-penetrate "encrypted" networks and switched to noncommercial "open source" software like eDonkey and BitTorrent.

There is no doubt that file sharing has become more difficult in the wake of the RIAA lawsuits. Aside from the obvious intimidation factor, there are roadblocks and booby traps. By now it is common knowledge that up to 30 percent of the available files on the net are spoofs, or fake tracks planted by record companies. This assertion from the last chapter of *Playback* still stands: Illegal downloading requires patience, savvy, and a high-speed connection. Now we should add one more requirement: access to legal representation.

And the sole prediction I made in the last chapter has stood the test of time. Unsurprisingly, the compact disc has yet to disappear. In fact, prerecorded CD sales have slightly improved after several years of decline. According to Nielsen SoundScan, album sales were up nearly 7 percent in the first six months of 2004. There were 305 million total albums sold, compared to 286 million for the same period in 2003. One sobering note lingers, though: Sales still lag behind the year before (2002) by 2 percent. The boom years of the nineties are ancient history. At the same time, sales of legal music downloads have increased—dramatically. Taken together, the online music services average sales of more than 2 million a week. Fifty-four million songs were legally downloaded in the first six months of 2004. But the media hype overshadows the reality: The market size for legal downloads is extremely modest. Despite the aura of success surrounding the iTunes Music Store, legal downloads account for *one percent* of total recorded music sales.

Is this up-tick in CD sales a product of the RIAA lawsuits? Clearly, quite a few illegal file-sharers were deterred by the RIAA campaign. The Pew Internet and American Life Project survey, released in January 2004, suggests that the number of U.S. Internet users who download music has fallen dramatically:

> The percentage of online Americans downloading music files on the Internet dropped by half and the numbers who were downloading files on any given day plunged after the Recording Industry Association of America (RIAA) began filing suits against those suspected of copyright infringement. A nationwide phone survey of 1358 adult internet users showed that the percentage of music file downloaders had fallen to 14% (about 18 million) from 29% (about 35 million) six months previous.
>
> Furthermore, a fifth of those who say they continue to download or share files online say they are doing so less often because of the suits.

Of course, the reliability of such self-reported data is open to question. How many people will admit to breaking the law for the sake of a survey? Especially when you consider the threat of RIAA lawsuits, these results begin to reek of self-censorship. At the other end of the scale, Big Champagne's summer 2004 research showed that illegal file sharing has increased in the year since the RIAA began its plan of prosecution.

Right now we have to declare this bout a draw.

A crucial legal decision has helped to protect or even perpetuate file sharing, at least for the present time. In August 2004, the Ninth Circuit Court of Appeals ruled that Grokster and other peer-to-peer (file-sharing) services were legal because their software could also be used for legitimate purposes. The RIAA and Hollywood film studios protested this decision, making the perfectly reasonable point that most of the material shared on these services has been illegally copied. The Ninth Circuit was upholding the U.S. Supreme Court's Betamax decision: In 1984, the Court ruled in favor of Sony (makers of the Betamax video recorder) over the film and television studios who claimed home videotaping was a copyright violation. In October 2004, representatives of the entertainment industry requested that the Supreme Court overturn the Ninth Circuit Court's ruling.

A legal sanction on the very machines that enable file sharing may be the entertainment industry's next move. Currently being considered by the U.S. Senate, the Inducing Infringement of Copyrights Act (SB2560) was introduced in June 2004. The chief sponsor is Senator Orrin Hatch (R-Utah), head of the Senate Judiciary Committee. The bipartisan group of supporters includes such unlikely allies as Senate Minority Leader Thomas Daschle (D-South Dakota) and Senate Majority Leader Bill Frist (R-Tennessee). Under the act, anyone who "aids, abets, induces, procures" unauthorized copyright material is held liable. So when the RIAA sues a KaZaA user, say, the manufacturer of any product used in that file-sharing process—software and hardware—

faces a secondary liability. Opponents of the act, mostly tech companies and consumer groups, claim the so-called Induce Act is so broadly worded that *any* electronic device that promotes copying of digital content is threatened: personal computers, iPods and other digital music players, CD burners, DVD players, VCRs, and Tivo. By its very nature, the Induce Act seeks to modernize—or undermine—the Supreme Court's Betamax decision. The lines in the sand have been drawn.

In the midst of all this litigation, a controversial study by two economics professors raised questions about the basic assumptions behind the RIAA's entire anti-piracy crusade. Felix Oberholzer-Gee, associate professor at the Harvard Business School, and Koleman Stumpf, associate professor at the University of North Carolina, tracked sales of 680 albums over the course of seventeen weeks in the second half of 2002. Matching that data with file-sharing activity on the OpenNap network, they observed that file sharing actually increased CD sales for albums that sell more than 600,000 copies, that is, hit albums.

"Our hypothesis was that if downloads are killing music, then albums that are downloaded more intensively should sell less," said Strumpf. Amazingly, the opposite results emerged. "It's a finding that surprised us," Oberholzer-Gee told the *Harvard University Gazette*. "We just couldn't document a negative relationship between file sharing and music sales." The RIAA and many other industry analysts scoffed at the study, dismissing it as an eccentric academic fluke. Yet it seems entirely plausible that even voracious downloaders wouldn't *totally* stop buying CDs. In this model, file sharing complements and encourages CD sales. Users sample a wide range of (free) music via downloading, and then actually buy the entire albums (including packaging and information) by their favorites. Here's another not-so-bold prediction: Prerecorded CDs will stick around a while longer.

Along with the technology challenge, however, the music industry faces a widening generation gap. In the twentieth century, young people listened to rebellious music. In the twenty-first century they listen to music in rebellious ways. There's a deeper reason why teenagers and college students, more than anyone else, still traffic in illegitimate MP3 files. Free music is only part of the allure. File sharing is forbidden, communal, insular, clandestine, and uncommonly cool. Downloading is the new rock and roll; for devotees the very act of file sharing becomes an expression of cultural rebellion. This should come as no surprise: The first hip-hop generation, raised on the sounds of samples and bites, views the whole notion of intellectual property rights in a radically different way than their parents do.

Downloading will never go away; it can only be contained. But in the end, the downside of illegal file sharing is inescapable. The risks begin to outweigh the benefits. After all, most people don't want to live outside the law. It gets too complicated.

## The Looming Format War

Let's reconsider the very first sentence of *Playback*: "Suddenly, popular music resembles an alien landscape." In 2004, the alien landscape—where people download recorded music from the Internet—feels more and more like familiar territory. Look at the most obvious example: Those white ear buds you see all around were just beginning to sprout when the hardcover edition was finished. And now, after three years on the market, Apple's portable digital player already seems ubiquitous. Sleek and efficient, the iPod has become an icon, maybe even a cliché. At this point its very name works as a genre-defining brand like Coca-Cola—or the Victrola.

In other words, the iPod rules, OK? Analysts say the iPod has more than a 50 percent share of the market for hard disk–based audio players. More than 4 million of these slim, pocket-size players had been sold by mid 2004, with 1.7 million sold in the first six months of 2004 alone. And 70 million songs were sold on iTunes Music Store site during its first year of operation.

Even as it struggles with a tiny share of the personal computer market, Apple is busy remaking itself as a music company. iPods are selling at a rate of about $1 billion a year and account for more than 12 percent of Apple's revenue. Hardware profits from iPod carry software losses on iTunes. And iPod sales helped boost the company's third-quarter profits in 2004 by a whopping 30 percent over the previous year.

"We basically make only a little bit of money on [iTunes]— we break even to make a little bit of profit, somewhere in that range," Apple chief executive Steve Jobs told the BBC. "And we're the largest by far. So everyone else must be losing money. I don't know what people that don't have an iPod business are doing because there's not a lot of money to be made running an online music store."

That hasn't stopped anybody from trying. Thanks to iTunes' piggyback ride on the accelerating success of the iPod, the competition amid online music stores is heating up. A shakeout seems inevitable, but it hasn't happened yet. Microsoft and Sony, slow to enter the fray, are now mounting the most serious challenges to Apple's dominance. And a slew of services have been bucking against iTunes since the beginning: Online offerings from Yahoo, Real Networks, the legalized Napster (now owned by Roxio), Wal-Mart, MusicMatch, BuyMusic, eMusic, and others have been met with only middling response from consumers. Lurking on the sidelines are subscription sites like Real's moderately popular Rhapsody, which offers streaming and CD burning but no actual downloads.

But the success of the iPod, arguably the biggest triumph in music technology since Peter Goldmark invented the LP, could quickly turn into a disaster for the emerging digital music scene. A full-scale format war may now be inevitable, due mostly to Steve Jobs' intransigence. A lack of compatibility between the competing portable players threatens to cripple the entire digital music market. Playing hardball with iPod's challengers could ultimately backfire for Jobs and Apple. The problem in a nutshell: Only music downloaded through iTunes will play on iPods, and iTunes music won't play on any portable device except an iPod. Apple refuses to license its technology to third parties.

"The iPod already works with the number one music service in the world and the iTunes music store works with the number one digital music player in the world," said Jobs. "The number twos are so far behind already. Why would we want to work with a number two?"

Without basic compatibility between formats, confusion reigns and consumers grow hesitant about the new technology. Then the whole business suffers, and development grinds to a halt. That was the lesson of the Battle of the Speeds in the late 1940s, which RCA and Columbia learned the hard way. Wisely, they cooperated in the end, making their mutually exclusive formats—33 and 45 rpm records—adaptable to any record player. Incredible as it may seem, the iPod could wind up a loser in the currently looming war—the digital equivalent of an 8-track tape player or a Betamax video recorder.

The first skirmish in the iPod war flared up during 2004. After Steve Jobs rejected a personal appeal from Real Network's chief executive to include his firm's music on iPods, Rob Glaser refused to take no for an answer. He instructed Real Network's engineers to penetrate the proprietary digital rights management (DRM) format used by the iPod. And they managed to crack the code. Real Network developed a technology called Harmony, effectively circumventing Apple's ironically named FairPlay DRM format. DRM is a copy-protection technology that limits how a song purchased through iTunes (or any online service) can be duplicated. Despite the iPod's rapid rise, Glaser told the *Washington Post* that online music won't really take off until standards are established that make it possible to hear any file on any device—just like CDs and DVDs.

"There's a format war," he said.

One feature on the iPod that's worth noting is its ability to copy and store all the music files on another iPod. In essence, you can peruse a friend's music library, and also open up your own collection for browsing and borrowing. The iPod also allows users to stream (listen to) other iPod users' libraries over a network (like the iTunes Music Store). Here's yet another cautious prediction: Gradually, the personal play list will replace the album as the organizing principle and basic currency of pop music exchange. There's a huge opportunity here for savvy record companies; downloading songs over the Internet can become as addictive as eating potato chips. One track inevitably links to a hunger for more and more and more. As we've seen all along, the very nature of the Net—diverse and data-saturated— encourages musical tastes to expand and grow exponentially.

In fact, many of the patterns and precedents charted in *Playback* keep coming back to haunt us. A developer who worked on the iPod recently made the unsurprising claim that Steve Jobs was personally involved in every mundane detail of the project. According to Ben Knauss' quite credible testimony, once the basic iPod prototypes were built, Jobs peppered the designers and engineers with daily queries and demands. One result of Jobs' micromanaging should sound eerily familiar, as it's a direct echo of his forebear Thomas Edison. The iPod is louder than most MP3 players because Jobs is partially deaf, Knauss told *Wired News*. "They drove the sound up so he [Jobs] could hear it," he said.

One thing is certain: Before this century is over, the mighty iPod will sound as primitive and quaint as Thomas Edison's cylinder phonograph does now. What goes around comes around.

# SELECT BIBLIOGRAPHY

## Books

Brewster, Bill, and Frank Broughton. *Last Night a DJ Saved My Life: The History of the DJ*. Grove Press, 1999.

Buskin, Richard. *Inside Tracks*. Spike, 1999.

Chanan, Michael. *Repeated Takes*. Verso, 1995.

Chapple, Steve, and Reebee Garofalo. *Rock & Roll Is Here to Pay*. Nelson-Hall, 1978.

Clark, Dick, and Richard Robinson. *Rock, Roll & Remember*. Popular Library, 1978.

Cohn, Nik. *Rock from the Beginning*. Pocket Books, 1970.

Cunningham, Mark. *Good Vibrations: A History of Record Production*. Sanctuary Music Library, 1998.

Dannen, Frederic. *Hit Men*. Times Books, 1990.

Dawson, Jim. *The Twist*. Faber & Faber, 1995.

Eisen, Jonathan, ed. *The Age of Rock*. Random House, 1969.

Eisenberg, Evan. *The Recording Angel*. McGraw-Hill, 1987.

Fricke, Jim, and Charlie Ahearn. *Yes Yes Y'all: The Experience Music Project Oral History of Hip Hop*. Da Capo Press, 2002.

Gelatt, Roland. *The Fabulous Phonograph 1877–1977*. Macmillan, 1977.

George, Nelson. *The Death of Rhythm & Blues*. Dutton, 1989.

Glinsky, Albert. *Theremin: Ether Music and Espionage*. University of Illinois Press, 2000.

Goldman, Albert. *Disco*. Hawthorn, 1978.

Goldmark, Peter C. *Maverick Inventor: My Turbulent Years at CBS*. Saturday Review Press, 1973.

Gracyk, Tim. *Popular American Recording Pioneers 1895–1925.* Haworth, 2000.

Griffith, Nancy, and Kim Masters. *Hit and Run.* Simon & Schuster, 1996.

Haden-Guest, Anthony. *The Last Party.* Morrow, 1997.

Handley, Susannah. *Nylon: Story of a Fashion Revolution.* Johns Hopkins University Press, 1999.

Harvith, John, and Susan Edwards. *Edison, Musicians and the Phonograph.* Greenwood Press, 1987.

Hebdige, Dick. *Cut & Mix.* Comedia, 1997.

Israel, Paul. *Edison: A Life of Invention.* Wiley, 1998.

Jackson, John A. *Big Beat Heat: Alan Freed and the Early Years of Rock & Roll.* Schirmer Books, 1991.

———. *American Bandstand: Dick Clark and the Making of a Rock & Roll Empire.* Oxford, 1997.

Johnstone, Bob. *We Were Burning: Japanese Entrepreneurs and the Forging of the Electronic Age.* Basic Books, 1999.

Kraft, Joseph P. *From Stage to Studio: Musicians and the Sound Revolution 1890–1950.* Johns Hopkins University Press, 1996.

Kurzweil, Ray. *The Age of Spiritual Machines.* Viking/Penguin, 1999.

Lanza, Joseph. *Elevator Music.* Picador, 1994.

Malone, Bill C., and Judith McCulloh, eds. *Stars of Country Music.* University of Illinois Press, 1975.

Martin, George. *All You Need Is Ears.* St. Martin's Press, 1979.

Millard, Andre. *America on Record: A History of Recorded Sound.* Cambridge University Press, 1995.

Moore, Jerrold Northup. *Sound Revolution: A Biography of Fred Gaisberg, Founding Father of Commercial Sound Recording.* Sanctuary Music Library, 1999.

Nasaw, David. *Going Out: The Rise and Fall of Public Amusement.* Basic Books, 1987.

Passman, Arnold. *The Deejays: How the Tribal Chieftains of Radio Got to Where They're At.* Macmillan, 1971.

Perry, Dick. *Not Just a Sound: The Story of WLW.* Prentice-Hall, 1971.

Poschardt, Ulf. *DJ Culture.* Quartet Books, 1998.

Read, Oliver, and Walter L. Welch. *From Tinfoil to Stereo: Evolution of the Phonograph.* Howard Sams, 1976.

Reynolds, Simon. *Generation Ecstasy.* Little, Brown, 1998.

Rose, Tricia. *Black Noise: Rap Music and Black Culture in Contemporary America.* Wesleyan University Press, 1994.

Roxon, Lillian. *Rock Encyclopedia.* Grosset's Universal Library, 1971.

Sanjek, Russell, and David Sanjek. *The American Popular Music Business in the 20th Century.* Oxford, 1984.

Shapiro, Peter, ed. *Modulations: A History of Electronic Music Throbbing Words on Sound.* Distributed Art Publishers/Caipirinha, 2000.

Shaughnessy, Mary Alice. *Les Paul: An American Original.* William Morrow, 1993.

Standage, Tom. *The Victorian Internet.* Walker, 1998.

Stokes, Geoffrey. *Starmaking Machinery.* Vintage, 1977.

Stolzoff, Norman. *Wake the Town and Tell the People: Dancehall Culture in Jamaica.* Duke University Press, 2000.

Toop, David. *Rap Attack 2: African Rap to Global Hip-Hop.* Serpent's Tail, 1991.

Tosches, Nick. *Country.* Scribners, 1985.

Valin, Jonathan. *The Music Lovers.* Dell, 1994.

Warhol, Andy. *The Andy Warhol Diaries.* Edited by Pat Hackett. Warner, 1989.

Welch, Walter L., and Leah Burt. *From Tinfoil to Stereo.* University of Florida Press, 1984.

Whitburn, Joel. *Pop Memories 1890–1954.* Record Research, 1986.

———. *The Billboard Book of Top 40 Albums.* Billboard Books, 1987.

———. *The Billboard Book of Top 40 Hits.* Billboard Books, 1989.

———. *Top 40 R&B Singles 1942–1988.* Record Research, 1989.

Whitcomb, Ian. *After the Ball.* Simon & Schuster, 1973.

Wolfe, Tom. *The Kandy Kolored Tangerine Flake Streamline Baby.* Pocket, 1970.

## Introduction and Chapter One

### Articles

Baruck, Lauren. "Napster Plug Pulled as Judge Blocks Bid." *New York Post*, 9 September 2002.

# Select Bibliography

Eds. "100 Years of Sound Reproduction." *High Fidelity* 27, no. 1 (January 1977).

Forman, Bill, ed. "The Father of Invention: Special Commemorative Issue." *NARAS Journal* 8, no. 1 (Winter–Spring 1997–98).

Goldsmith, Charles, and Jennifer Ordonez. "Levy Jolts EMI: Can He Reform Music Industry?" *Wall Street Journal*, 6 September 2002.

Gundersen, Edna. "Anyway You Spin It, the Music Biz Is in Trouble." *USA Today*, 5 June 2002.

Harrington, Richard. "Putting It on the Record." *Washington Post*, 26 December 1999.

Holson, Laura M. "With by-the-Numbers Radio, Requests Are a Dying Breed." *New York Times*, 11 July 2002.

Koerner, Brendan I. "Mr. Roboto: When Pols Attack." *Village Voice*, 30 July 2002.

Mathews, Anna Wilde. "A Giant Radio Chain Is Perfecting the Art of Seeming Local." *Wall Street Journal*, 2002.

McDonough, John. "The Day the Music Died." *Wall Street Journal*, 31 July 2002.

Mossberg, Walter S. "Groovin' with Portable Jukeboxes." *Wall Street Journal*, 19 June 2002.

Riordan, Teresa. "Historians Take a Longer View of Net Battles." *New York Times*, 10 April 2000.

Rothstein, Edward. "Pursuing 'Real' Sound, with Artifice as the Ideal." *New York Times*, 11 March 2000.

Strauss, Neil. "Behind the Grammys, Revolt in the Industry." *New York Times*, 24 February 2002.

Thomas, Paulette. "Clack. Clack. The Typewriter's Back?" *Wall Street Journal*, 14 November 2000.

Weinraub, Bernard. "For the Industry, Less to Celebrate at the Grammys." *New York Times*, 25 February 2002.

Wolff, Michael. "Facing the Music." *New York Magazine*, 10 June 2002.

Wondrich, David. "Ragtime: No Longer a Novelty in Sepia." *New York Times*, 21 January 2001.

Zwick, Edward. "How Al Edison Surmounted the Heartbreak of Excessive Dandruff and Went on to Become the Father of the Gramophone." *Rolling Stone*, 27 September 1973.

## Internet

National Inventors Hall of Fame: www.invent.org/
The Player Piano Page: www.pianola.demon.co.uk
U.S. Patent Office: www.uspto.gov/
UK Patent Office: www.patent.gov.uk/patent/

## Chapter Two

### Articles

Dreazen, Yochi J. "Pittsburgh's KDKA Tells Story of How Radio Has Survived." *Wall Street Journal*, 15 May 2001.
Eds. "100 Years of Sound Reproduction." *High Fidelity* 27, no. 1 (January 1977).
Forman, Bill, ed. "The Father of Invention: Special Commemorative Issue." *NARAS Journal* 8, no. 1 (Winter–Spring 1997–98).
Miller, Chuck. "America's Musicians Contribute to the War Effort via V-Disc Records." *Goldmine*, 29 January 1999.

## Chapter Three

### Articles

Hamilton, David. "To the LP at 40! Hail! (And Farewell?)" *New York Times*, 5 June 1988.
"Peter Goldmark 1906–1977." *Rolling Stone*, 26 January 1978.
Zwick, Edward. "An Interview with the Father of Hi-Fi: Dr. Peter Goldmark." *Rolling Stone*, 27 September 1973.

## Chapter Four

### Articles

Angwin, Julia. "Web Radio Showdown." *Wall Street Journal*, 15 May 2002.

Dreazen, Yochi J. "Pittsburgh's KDKA Tells Story of How Radio Has Survived." *Wall Street Journal*, 15 May 2001.

Dreazen, Yochi J., and Anna Wilde Matthews. "Senators Focus on Reach, Clout of Radio Giant." *Wall Street Journal*, 27 January 2003.

Feder, Barnaby. "A New Temptation for the Ears, via Satellite." *New York Times*, 2 June 2002.

Holson, Laura M. "With by-the-Numbers Radio, Requests Are a Dying Breed." *New York Times*, 11 July 2002.

Johnston, Nicholas. "Wider Loss, Longer Subscriber List at XM Satellite Radio." *Washington Post*, 9 May 2003.

Knippel, Jim. "On the Air." *New York Press*, 29 August 2001.

Koda, Cub. *The Best of Freddie "Boom-Boom" Cannon*. CD liner notes. Rhino, 1995.

Mathews, Anna Wilde. "How Technology Changed the Way We Listen to the Radio." *Wall Street Journal*, 13 November 2000.

———. "A Giant Radio Chain Is Perfecting the Art of Seeming Local." *Wall Street Journal*, 25 February 2002.

Mathews, Anna Wilde, and Jennifer Ordonez. "Music Labels Say It Costs Too Much to Get Songs on Radio." *Wall Street Journal*, 10 June 2002.

"New Format for Radio: All Digital." *New York Times*, 25 January 2001.

Nolan, Tom. "Underground Radio." In Jonathan Eisen, ed., *The Age of Rock*. Random House, 1969.

"RCA Victor Portable Automatic 'Victrola' $39.95" (Advertisement). *High Fidelity* (February 1957): 59.

Shearer, Harry. "Captain Pimple Cream's Fiendish Plot." In Jonathan Eisen, ed., *The Age of Rock*. Random House, 1969.

"Sparks Still Fly in Format Fracas." *Billboard*, 15 December 1958.

Taub, Eric. "Drive-Time Radio on 100 Channels." *New York Times*, 19 October 2000.

"The Columbia 360." *High Fidelity* (March–April 1953): 82–83.

## Chapter Five

### Articles

Chusid, Irwin. "Joe Meek's Musical Rocket Science." *DISCoveries* (August 1996).

Hunter, Mark. "The Beat Goes off: How Technology Has Gummed up Rock's Grooves." *Harper's* (May 1987).

Kaye, Lenny. "Les Paul: Creator of the Electric Guitar and the New Sound." *Goldmine*, 29 January 1999.

Lanza, Joseph. "Whitebread Rhapsody." *New York Press*, 12–18 May 1999.

McCready, John. "Room at the Top" (Joe Meek profile). *Mojo* (May 2001).

Page, Tim. "LP at 50: Waxing Nostalgic." *Washington Post*, 18 January 1998.

Tyler, Kieron. "Adventures in Stereo." *Mojo* (August 2000).

## Chapter Six

### Articles

Aletti, Vince. "Dancing Madness." *Rolling Stone*, 28 August 1975.

Bergman, Barrie. "Carving Up the Golden Goose." *Billboard*, 6 October 1979.

"Black Music: A Genealogy of Sound." *Billboard*, 9 September 1979.

Braunstein, Peter. "Disco." *American Heritage*, November 1999.

Caviano, Ray. "Tiptoeing to the Disco Beat." *Billboard*, 2 June 1979.

"Chicago's WLUP Cools Attack on Rival Station." *Billboard*, 28 July 1979.

Grein, Paul. "Everybody's Jumping on the Disco Bandwagon." *Billboard*, 18 April 1979.

Joe, Radcliffe. "Dearth of Superstars Dims Industry Future." *Billboard*, 14 July 1979.

Kopkind, Andrew. "The Dialectics of Disco: Gay Music Goes Straight." *Village Voice*, 13 February 1979.

Kornbluth, Jesse. "Merchandising Disco for the Masses." *New York Times*, 13 February 1979.

Lichtman, Irv. "Cassettes Gaining in U.S." *Billboard*, 8 December 1979.

Mackinnon, Angus. "Der Munich Mensch Machine—Giorgio Moroder." *New Musical Express*, 9 and 16 December 1978.

"Music to Move to: Disco: A Billboard Supplement." *Billboard*, 1 November 1975.

Strauss, Neil. "Francis Grasso, 52, 60s DJ and Master of the Club Mix." (Obituary.) *New York Times*, 25 March 2001.

Traiman, Stephen. "Sony's Tiny Stereo Player." *Billboard*, 8 December 1979.

### Internet

Tom Moulton Tribute Page: www.disco-disco.com/tributes/tom.html

## Chapter Seven

### Articles

Allen, Harry. "Why Sugar Hill Records Matters." Liner notes. *The Sugar Hill Records Story*. Rhino, 1997.

Beresford, Steve. "Cut Above the Rest: A Brief History of Dub." *Resonance* 2, no. 2 (n.d.).

Farber, Jim. "A Team of DJ Veterans Busily Turning Tables." *New York Daily News*, 12 March 2002.

Ford, Robert, Jr. "Jive Talking NY DJs Rapping Away in Black Discos." *Billboard*, 5 May 1979.

George, Nelson. "Hip Hop History: Founding Fathers Speak the Truth." *The Source*, November 1993.

George, Nelson, and Brian Chin. "The Sylvia Robinson Story." *Record World*, 1 August 1981.

Heibutzki, Ralph. "Time Enough for the Old School: The Hip Hop Revolution 1970–1990." *Goldmine*, 24 May 1996.

Hodgkinson, Will. "Spin City." *The Guardian*, 2 September 2002.

Houston, Frank. "Gather Round the Electronic Piano." *New York Times*, 16 December 1999.

Hundley, Jessica. "Interview: DJ Qbert." *New York Press*, 21–27 February 2001.

Nossiter, Adam. "Hip-Hop Club (Gang?) Is Banned in the Bronx: Cultural Questions About Zulu Nation." *New York Times*, 4 October 1995.

Sockwell-Mason, Ikimulisa. "Farrakhan: Rappers Scare White Parents." *New York Post*, 14 June 2001.

Strauss, Neil. "The Battle of the Needle Freaks." *Spin*, 1999.

Toop, David. *Tommy-Boy's Greatest Beats*. CD box liner notes. 1998.

Werde, William. "The Real Spin Doctors." *Washington Post*, 7 February 1999.

## Chapter Eight

### Articles

Barrett, Todd. "The Start of a CD Backlash?" *Newsweek*, 16 July 1990.

Browne, David. "A Vinyl Farewell." *Entertainment Weekly*, 4 Ocotber 1991.

Christman, Ed. "Retailers Call for Lower CD Prices: Shamrock CEO Irks Labels at NARM." *Billboard*, 24 March 1990.

Ehrlichman, James. "Sudden Death of the Long-Playing Record." *Manchester Guardian Weekly*, 17 March 1991.

Farhi, Paul. "Compact Discs Turn Tables on Vinyl Record Sales." *Washington Post*, 14 March 1989.

Fremer, Michael. "Fans Flock to Vinyl in the Era of CDs." *New York Times*, 7 July 1998.

"Janus of the Turntable." *Economist*, 11 August 1990.

Meltzer, Richard. "Buy a VTR and Rule the World." *Village Voice*, 13 November 1978.

Morris, Edward. "Virginia Retailer Steps up Drive to Lower CD Prices." *Billboard*, 17 March 1990.

Pollack, Andrew. "Akio Morita, Key to Japan's Rise as Co-Founder of Sony, Dies at 78." *New York Times*, 3 October 1999.

Popson, Tom. "Counter Intelligence—Launching an All-Vinyl Record Store in the '90s." *Chicago Tribune*, 13 April 1990.

Segal, David. "They Sell the Whole World Songs: Mass Merchants Offer Convenience." *Washington Post*, 21 February 2001.

Strauss, Neil. "For Record Industry, All Signs Are Gloomy." *New York Times*, 4 December 1996.

Terry, Ken, and Dave Dimartino. "Vinyl's Demise Accelerated by Label No-Return Policies." *Billboard*, 24 February 1990.

## Chapter Nine

### Articles

Ahrens, Frank. "Apple's Different Tune: Jobs Sells Music Service as Solution to Piracy." *Washington Post*, 29 April 2003.

———. "Song Sharers Get an Instant Scolding." *Washington Post*, 30 April 2003.

"Airplay." (System III Sirius Turntable.) *Wired*, October 2000.

Anderman, Joan. "Singled Out: Technology Has Put Users in Control, and Made Full-Length Albums Obsolete." *Baltimore Sun*, 4 July 2000.

Ante, Spencer E. "Inside Napster." *Business Week*, 14 August 2000.

Arango, Tim. "Apple Peeling Off." *New York Post*, 9 June 2003.

Barack. Lauren. "Apple's New iTunes Falls Prey to Piracy." *New York Post*, 15 May 2003.

———. "Music Biz Subpoenas 150 Users." *New York Post*, 17 July 2003.

———. "Subpoenas Sent to 870 Music File Bootleggers." *New York Post*, 22 July 2003.

Barlow, John Perry. "The Next Economy of Ideas." *Wired*, October 2000.

Berenson, Alex, and Matt Richtel. "Heartbreakers, Dream Makers: Despite Digital Upstarts, Big Labels Still Rule the Music Industry." *New York Times*, 25 June 2000.

Berlind, William. "The Future in 30 Seconds: Listening to iTunes for Free." *New York Observer*, 12 June 2003.

Brinkley, Joel. "After 15 Years, the Music CD Faces an Upscale Competitor." *New York Times*, 28 July 1997.

———. "Disk vs. Disk: The Fight for the Ears of America." *New York Times*, 8 August 1999.

Cummings, Sue "The Flux in Pop Music Has a Distinctly Download Beat to It." *New York Times*, 22 September 1999.

Flynn, Laurie J. "Apple Offers Music Downloads with Unique Pricing." *New York Times*, 29 April 2003.

Fremer, Michael. "SACD and DVD-A: The Promise of a Better Sound . . . But for Whom?" *Pulse!* December 2001.

Gallagher, David F. "Napster Users Test File-Sharing Alternatives." *New York Times*, 20 July 2001.

Gallivan, Joseph. "Napster Working Against Deadline, Smart Bootleggers." *New York Post*, 6 March 2001.

Gallivan, Joseph, and Allyson Lieberman. "Shotgun Wedding: Napster's Deal with Foes May Be Too Late." *New York Post*, 6 June 2001.

Garrity, Brian. "Forecast: Physical Music Sales Top Out in 2002, Retail Prices Drop." *Billboard*, 19 August 2000.

Gomes, Lee. "Gnutella, New Music-Sharing Software, Rattles the CD Industry." *Wall Street Journal*, 4 May 2000.

———. "Entertainment World Has Flawed Crystal Ball." *Wall Street Journal*, 20 June 2000.

———. "Napster Ruling May Just Be the Overture." *Wall Street Journal*, 28 June 2000.

———. "Napster, Fighting for Survival, to Make Case Before Appeals Panel." *Wall Street Journal*, 2 October 2000.

———. "Entertainment Firms Target Gnutella." *Wall Street Journal*, 4 May 2001.

Gomes, Lee, and Anna Wilde Mathews. "Napster Suffers a Rout in Appeals Court." *Wall Street Journal*, 13 February 2001.

Harmon, Amy. "Potent Software Escalates Music Industry's Jitters." *New York Times*, 7 March 2000.

Heilemann, John. "David Boies: The *Wired* Interview." *Wired*, October 2000.

Holson, Laura M. "Conducting Music's Digital Shift: A Top Lobbyist Seeks Harmony in a Time of Discord." *New York Times*, 20 August 2001. (Profile of RIAA's Hilary Rosen.)

Howe, Jeff. "Net Loss: Music Industry Report Projects Huge Losses to Web Piracy." *Village Voice*, 30 May 2000.

Huhn, Mary. "Big Deal May Force Free-Music Fans to Flee." *New York Post*, 2 November 2000.

Jenkins, Holman W., Jr. "Let's Give It Up for Metallica." *Wall Street Journal*, 10 May 2000.

————. "How to Survive a Post-Napster Copyright Holocaust." *Wall Street Journal*, 6 September 2000.

Kirkpatrick, David D. "Thomas Middelhoff Has a Hunch." *New York Times Magazine*, 10 June 2001.

Klein, Alec. "Going Napster One Better." *Washington Post*, 25 February 2001.

Krim, Jonathan. "Recording Firms Win Copyright Ruling." *Washington Post*, 22 January 2003.

Kushner, David. "The Beat Goes On Line, and Sometimes It's Legal." *New York Times*, 17 June 1999.

Marriott, Michael. "In the Storage Race, Will Consumers Win?" *New York Times*, 5 April 2001.

————. "With Plenty to Shine and Spin, CDs Weave Tapestries of Data." *New York Times*, 23 September 1999.

————. "Hey Walkman: Time to Face the Music on a Chip." *New York Times*, 20 July 2000.

Mathews, Anna Wilde. "Can the Record Industry Beat Free Web Music?" *Wall Street Journal*, 20 June 2000.

Mathews, Anna Wilde, and Nick Wingfield. "Apple's Planned Music Service for Windows Draws Rivals." *Wall Street Journal*, 9 May 2003.

Mossberg, Walter S. "Record Labels Launch Two Feeble Services to Replace Napster." *Wall Street Journal*, 7 February 2002.

Musgrove, Mike. "RIAA Plans to Sue Music Swappers." *Washington Post*, 26 June 2003.

O'Harrow, Robert, Jr. "Music Industry Will Offer Some Songs On Line, for a Price." *Washington Post*, 25 July 2001.

Peers, Martin, and William Boston. "Sour Note: Plugging into the Web Is a Jarring Experience for the Music Industry." *Wall Street Journal*, 12 April 2001.

Powers, Ann. "Fans Go Interactive, and Popular Culture Feels the Tremors." *New York Times*, 20 September 2000.

Repsher, William S. "E-Music vs. Napster." *New York Press*, 31 January–6 February 2001.

Richtel, Matt. "Appellate Judges Back Limitations on Copying Music." *New York Times*, 13 February 2001.

————. "Aimster Heads Down a Path Already Taken by Napster." *New York Times*, 1 June 2001.

————. "Aggressive Strategy Brought on Inquiry of Recording Industry." *New York Times*, 22 October 2001.

————. "Apple Is Said to Be Entering E-Music Fray with Pay Service." *New York Times*, 28 April 2003.

Richtel, Matt, and David D. Kirkpatrick. "In a Shift, Internet Service Will Pay for Music Rights." *New York Times*, 1 November 2000.

Sorkin, Andrew Ross. "Software Bullet Is Sought to Kill Music Piracy." *New York Times*, 4 May 2003.

Strauss, Neil. "Foraging for Music in the Digital Jungle." *New York Times*, 20 August 2001.

Tam, Pui-Wing. "Apple Launches Online Store Offering Downloadable Music." *Wall Street Journal*, 29 April 2003.

Tam, Pui-Wing, Bruce Orwall, and Anna Wilde Mathews. "As Apple Stalls, Steve Jobs Looks to Digital Entertainment." *Wall Street Journal*, 25 April 2003.

Taub, Eric A. "New Ways for Discs and Heads to Spin." *New York Times*, 17 May 2001.

Toomey, Jenny. "Hear Me Play, but Respect My Rights." *Washington Post*, 4 June 2000.

Viega, Alex. "File-Sharing Dips After Threat to Sue." *Washington Post*, 15 July 2003.

Waldemar, Patti, Andrew Heavens, and Christopher Grimes. "Copyright Ruling May Close Napster Song-Swap Website." *Financial Times*, 27 July 2000.

Weintraub, Arlene. "MP3.Com Faces the Music." *Business Week*, 9 April 2001.

Wingfield, Nick. "Napster Boy, Interrupted." *Wall Street Journal*, 4 October 2002.

————. "Students Settle File-Sharing Suit; Each to Pay Recording Industry." *Wall Street Journal*, 1 May 2003.

Wingfield, Nick, and Anna Wilde Mathews. "Online Music Goes Mainstream." *Wall Street Journal*, 29 November 2001.

# INDEX

# Index

# Index

## Index

# Index

# Index

# Index

# Index

# Index

# Index